THE BUSY DAY DINNERS COOKBOOK

STACIE VAUGHAN & RANDA DERKSON

ISBN 978-1-0691509-0-5

First printing December 2024

Visit the author's website: https://busydaydinners.com
For more information, please contact hello@busydaydinners.com

For my partner, Veldon, whose unwavering support has made this journey possible—I'm endlessly grateful for you. To my daughters, Olivia and Bridget, who inspire me every day—I love you all more than words can express. And to my cherished cats, Misty and Reggie, and in loving memory of my sweet Princess, who will always hold a special place in my heart, thank you for the comfort and joy you bring to my life.

Stacie

To my children, Carter and Vivienne, for eating what I made... most of the time. This cookbook is dedicated to your bravery in trying new things and your blunt reviews when it didn't go well. Thanks for keeping me humble and eager to create picky eater approved recipes. Mommy loves you.

For my husband, Eric, who supports me in all my stress-induced madness, new projects, and for never once questioning why the kitchen looks like a tornado hit. I love and appreciate you.

Randa

Table of Contents

Introduction

Welcome to Busy Day Dinners! We know firsthand how hectic life can get, and when your schedule is packed, finding time to cook a delicious meal can feel like a challenge.

That's why we created this cookbook—to help you get tasty, satisfying dinners on the table without the stress. Whether you're juggling work, family, or just need a quick meal that doesn't require hours in the kitchen, this collection of recipes is here to make your evenings easier and more enjoyable.

In Busy Day Dinners, you'll find a variety of recipes that are big on flavor but simple to prepare. From hearty casseroles to vibrant sheet pan meals, from comforting pasta dishes to quick and tasty chicken dinners, there's something here for every craving and every kind of busy day. Each recipe is designed to be straightforward, using everyday ingredients that you probably already have in your pantry.

We've included a mix of classics and new favorites, with plenty of options to suit different tastes and occasions. Whether you're cooking for the family, hosting friends, or just looking for a quick weeknight meal, these recipes are all about making your life easier while still delivering on taste.

So, take a deep breath, relax, and let's make dinner time something you look forward to. With this cookbook, you'll have a collection of go-to recipes that you can rely on, no matter how busy your day has been.

Let's get cooking, and enjoy some stress-free, delicious meals together!

xo, Randa & Stacie

Cook Book Tips

This cookbook is designed to make your life easier by providing a variety of delicious, easy-to-make recipes that fit into your busy schedule. Here's a quick guide to help you navigate the book, understand how the chapters are organized, and get the most out of your cooking experience.

Chapter Organization

Busy Day Dinners is divided into chapters based on the type of meal, making it easy to find exactly what you're in the mood for. Whether you're looking for quick weeknight pasta dishes, hearty casseroles, or sheet pan dinners, you'll find a chapter dedicated to each category. The chapters are thoughtfully arranged so you can flip through and quickly find recipes that suit your needs, whether you have just 30 minutes to cook or want to plan ahead.

Reading the Recipes

Each recipe in this cookbook is laid out in a clear, easy-to-follow format:

- **Recipe Title:** At the top of each page, you'll find the name of the recipe.
- **Introduction**: Below the title, there's a brief introduction that provides context for the dish, offers serving suggestions, or shares a tip to make the cooking process smoother.
- **Ingredients List:** The ingredients are listed in the order they're used in the recipe. This helps you gather everything you need before you start cooking. Where possible, ingredients are kept simple and accessible, with notes on substitutions if you don't have something on hand.
- **Instructions:** The steps are written in a straightforward manner, guiding you through the cooking process from start to finish. Each step is designed to be easy to follow, even for beginner cooks, with tips included along the way to ensure success.
- **Prep and Cook Times:** These times are provided at the top of each recipe, so you can quickly gauge how long the dish will take from start to finish.

Make the Most of Busy Day Dinners

Meal Planning: Use the chapters to plan your meals for the week. You can mix and match recipes from different chapters to create a balanced menu, or focus on one chapter for a themed week of dinners.

Prep Ahead: Look for recipes that can be prepped ahead of time, especially on weekends. This will save you time during the week and make dinner a breeze on those extra busy nights.

Flexible Cooking: Don't hesitate to make substitutions based on what you have in your pantry or what's in season. Many recipes are adaptable, and the tips throughout the book will help you customize dishes to suit your taste.

Utilize Leftovers: Some recipes yield leftovers that can be repurposed for another meal. Check the notes for ideas on how to use them in creative ways, reducing food waste and making the most of your cooking.

Get Inspired: Flip through the beautiful photos to get inspired! Sometimes, just seeing a dish can spark an idea for what to cook next. The visual appeal of each recipe is meant to entice and motivate you to try something new.

With Busy Day Dinners, the goal is to make your cooking experience enjoyable, efficient, and rewarding. Use this guide to navigate the book with ease, and let the recipes help you create delicious, stress-free meals for you and your family.

Author's Note:

Creating Busy Day Dinners has been a labor of love for both of us, inspired by our own hectic day to days as busy moms, business owners, and home cooks. We know that even on the worst days, a home-cooked meal can bring comfort, connection, and a sense of calm amidst the chaos. This cookbook is our way of sharing that moment of peace with you.

Between the two of us, we bring decades of cooking experience and a deep passion for making meals that are both delicious and approachable. Our journeys started in our kitchens, where we discovered the joy of creating simple, satisfying dishes that our families loved. As life got busier, we realized the importance of having a repertoire of go-to recipes that are quick to prepare but still feel special.

Busy Day Dinners is a collection of those recipes—meals that you can count on when time is tight, but you still want to serve something homemade, nourishing, and delicious.

Whether it's a quick pasta dish after a long day, a comforting casserole that feeds the whole family, or a flavorful sheet pan dinner with minimal cleanup, these recipes are designed to make your life easier and your dinners more enjoyable.

We hope this cookbook becomes a trusted resource in your kitchen, helping you create meals that bring joy to your table, even on the busiest of days.

From our kitchens to yours, thank you for allowing us to share these recipes with you. Happy cooking!

Meal Planning Tips

Meal planning is a game-changer for busy weeks. Not only does it save time and reduce stress, but it also helps you make healthier choices and avoid the last-minute scramble for dinner ideas. Here are some practical tips to help you plan your meals for the week, streamline your grocery shopping, make the most of leftovers, and create a balanced menu that keeps everyone satisfied.

- **Start with a weekly menu:** Set aside time each week to plan your meals. Consider your schedule. Are there nights when you'll be too busy to cook? On those days, opt for quick and easy recipes, or plan to use leftovers. Aim to include a variety of proteins, vegetables, and grains to keep your meals balanced and interesting.

- **Keep it simple**: It's tempting to try new and complex recipes every day, but for a busy week, simplicity is key. Stick to a few go-to recipes that you know are quick, easy, and loved by your family. Incorporate one or two new dishes each week if you like, but don't overwhelm yourself.

- **Plan for leftovers:** Leftovers are your best friend when it comes to saving time. Plan meals that will provide enough leftovers for another dinner or lunch the next day. Casseroles, soups, and sheet pan dinners are excellent for this. You can also cook extra portions of proteins like chicken or beef, which can be repurposed into new dishes later in the week.

- **Make a detailed grocery list:** After planning, make a grocery list organized by category (produce, dairy, meats, etc.). This will make your shopping trip more efficient and help ensure you don't forget any key ingredients. Check your pantry, fridge, and freezer to see what you already have on hand, so you're only buying what you need.

- **Meal prep**: Consider setting aside time on the weekend to do meal prep. Chop vegetables, cook grains, and even prepare some complete meals that can be stored in the fridge or freezer. This prep work can save you alot of time on busy nights and makes it easier to stick to your meal plan.

- **Use a mix of fresh and pantry ingredients:** To keep your meals varied and ensure you're not running to the store every few days, plan to use a mix of fresh and pantry ingredients. Canned beans, pasta, rice, and frozen vegetables can be lifesavers when you're short on fresh produce. This approach also helps reduce food waste, as you'll have more flexibility in when you use certain ingredients.

- **Stay flexible:** Life happens, and sometimes even the best-laid plans need to be adjusted. Build some flexibility into your meal plan by having a few backup meals that are quick to prepare, like a simple pasta dish or a stir-fry with frozen vegetables. This way, if your day doesn't go as planned, you won't be scrambling for dinner ideas.

- **Balance your meals**: When planning your weekly menu, aim for a balance of proteins, carbs, and fats. Include a variety of colors and textures to keep meals visually appealing and nutritionally diverse. Consider incorporating meatless meals once or twice a week, which can keep it budget friendly.

- **Involve the family:** Involve your family in the meal planning process. Ask for input on what they'd like to eat during the week, which can help ensure that everyone is happy with the meals you prepare. It's also a great way to introduce kids to the idea of balanced eating and the planning process. Bonus points if they help with cooking!

- **Keep track of your favorites:** As you discover recipes that are hits with your family, keep a list of these favorites. Over time, you'll build a library of go-to meals that you can rely on, making future meal planning even easier.

By taking the time to plan your meals for the week, you'll find that dinner time becomes less stressful and more enjoyable.

Shortcuts & Time Saving Tips

When life gets busy, finding time to cook can feel like a challenge, so we're sharng some of our favorite shortcuts and time saving tips to make dinner time easier.

- **Use pre-cooked chicken:** Whether you cook up chicken breasts in advance or buy a cooked rotisserie chicken from the grocery store, this saves a ton of time for recipes that use cooked chicken like Chicken Caesar Sandwiches (page 91) and our Chicken Pot Pie Casserole (page 129).
- **Buy pre-done sauces**: Not everything has to be homemade all the time. One of our favorite shortcuts is to purchase jarred marinara and pestos. Try them in our Pizza Ravioli (page 77) and our Pesto Stuffed Chicken (page 97).
- **Use microwaveable rice:** Another huge time saver is to use the bags of ready to eat rice for quick additions to bowls or as a side for your main dish.
- **Pre-cut vegetables:** If you have a bunch of vegetables to cut up, you can save time by grabbing them already done from the grocery store. We recommend pre-cut bags of broccoli for recipes like our Teriyaki Salmon with Broccoli (page 62) and our Chicken Ramen Stir Fry (page 103).
- **No-cook sides**: Everyone loves veggies and dip! If you're stressing over a side dish idea, go back to the party favorites and serve it with veggies and dip. Not everything has to be a gourmet meal. Fresh fruit and vegetables always hit the spot.
- **Prep for future busy days:** Do your future self a solid by doubling one of your favorite recipes and cook the second half in a seperate dish. Freeze it for another week.

Conversion Charts

Having the right measurements can make all the difference between a good meal and a great one. Whether you're adjusting a recipe to suit your needs, following a recipe from another country, or simply working with the ingredients you have on hand, these conversion charts are here to help. Use them as a quick reference to ensure that your dinners come out perfectly, no matter what you're cooking.

Volume Conversions

U.S. Standard to Metric

1 teaspoon = 5 milliliters (ml)
1 tablespoon = 15 milliliters (ml)
¼ cup = 60 milliliters (ml)
⅓ cup = 80 milliliters (ml)
½ cup = 120 milliliters (ml)
⅔ cup = 160 milliliters (ml)
3/4 cup = 180 milliliters (ml)
1 cup = 240 milliliters (ml)
1 pint = 480 milliliters (ml)
1 quart = 960 milliliters (ml)
1 gallon = 3.8 liters (L)

U.K. Imperial to Metric

1 teaspoon = 5 milliliters (ml)
1 tablespoon = 15 milliliters (ml)
1 fluid ounce = 28 milliliters (ml)
1 cup = 284 milliliters (ml)
1 pint = 568 milliliters (ml)
1 quart = 1.14 liters (L)
1 gallon = 4.55 liters (L)

Weight Conversions

U.S. Standard to Metric

1 ounce = 28 grams (g)
4 ounces = 113 grams (g)
8 ounces = 227 grams (g)
12 ounces = 340 grams (g)
1 pound = 454 grams (g)
2 pounds = 907 grams (g) or approximately 1 kilogram (kg)

Temperate Conversions

Fahrenheit to Celsius
250°F = 120°C
300°F = 150°C
325°F = 160°C
350°F = 180°C
375°F = 190°C
400°F = 200°C
425°F = 220°C
450°F = 230°C
475°F = 245°C
500°F = 260°C

Kitchen Tools

Sheet Pan/Baking Pan
Whether you're roasting veggies, making sheet pan dinners, or baking cookies, this versatile tool allows you to cook multiple ingredients at once. Line it with parchment paper or aluminum foil for easy clean up.

High-Quality Knives
A sharp, reliable chef's knife and a paring knife are absolute essentials. A good chef's knife will handle most of your chopping, slicing, and dicing, while a paring knife is perfect for smaller, more delicate tasks like peeling or mincing.

Cutting Board
A sturdy cutting board is a must have for prep. Look for one that's large enough to give you plenty of space to work, and consider having separate boards for meats and vegetables to avoid cross-contamination.

Mixing Bowls
A good set of mixing bowls are definite must haves. Stainless steel bowls are lightweight, durable, and don't retain odors, making them a great all-purpose option.

Measuring Cups and Spoons
Precision is key to many recipes, and a good set of measuring cups and spoons ensures you're using the right amounts of ingredients. Make sure to have both liquid and dry measuring cups.

Tongs
Whether you're grilling, frying, or tossing salads, a good pair of tongs gives you more control.

Casserole Dishes
Whether it's a casserole or lasagna, a good set of casserole dishes is essential for oven-based dinners. Glass or ceramic dishes are perfect for casseroles, roasts, and baked pastas.

Colander
Draining pasta, rinsing vegetables, or washing grains is much easier with a colander.

Kitchen Timer
Whether it's built into your oven, your phone, or a standalone gadget, a reliable kitchen timer ensures that you don't overcook or burn anything.

Garlic Press
If you love cooking with fresh garlic but hate the hassle of peeling and chopping, try a garlic press.

Large Skillet
A large skillet is perfect for everything from sautéing vegetables to searing meats and making one-pan meals. Its wide surface area allows for even cooking and gives you plenty of room to toss ingredients without overcrowding.

Scan to get Stacie & Randa's personal recommendations.
https://busydaydinners.com/resources

Beef Dinners

This collection of beef recipes is all about bringing big, bold flavors to your dinner table without spending hours in the kitchen. Whether you're in the mood for something quick and satisfying or a dish that feels like a warm hug after a long day, we've got you covered.

Start with the **Korean Ground Beef Bowls** *(21)* for a speedy weeknight meal that's packed with flavor. If you're in the mood for something comforting and hearty, the **Hearty Beef Chili** *(22)* or **One-Pot Ground Beef Stroganoff** *(27)* are sure to hit the spot.

These recipes are perfect for those days when you need something filling but don't want to spend all evening cooking.

For a fun twist on a classic, try the **Muffin Tin Meatloaf** *(28)* — a family favorite that's both easy and portion-perfect. And if you're craving something rich and savory, the **Salisbury Steak with Mushroom Gravy** *(31)* offers a nostalgic taste of comfort food done right.

The **Philly Cheesesteak Sloppy Joes** *(32)* bring all the flavors of a cheesesteak into a quick and easy sandwich that's perfect for busy nights. Meanwhile, the **Beef Burrito Bowls** *(35)* and **Ginger Beef Stir Fry** *(36)* offer fresh, vibrant options that are as tasty as they are simple to prepare.

Finally, don't miss the **Loaded Chili Baked Potato** *(25)*, a dish that combines the best of both worlds—creamy potatoes and hearty chili—for a meal that's sure to satisfy.

Each of these recipes is designed to help you get dinner on the table quickly, without sacrificing flavor or quality. So grab your ingredients, and let's dive into some delicious, stress-free cooking!

Korean Ground Beef Bowls

Savory beef, tangy cucumbers, and aromatic garlic come together over fluffy rice for a quick, 20-minute dinner that's bursting with flavor.

SERVES: 4 **PREP:** 5 MINUTES **COOK:** 15 MINUTES **TOTAL:** 20 MINUTES

1 pound lean ground beef
4 cloves garlic, minced
1 cup mini cucumbers, sliced
⅓ cup rice vinegar
⅓ cup soy sauce
¼ cup light brown sugar
1 ½ teaspoons toasted sesame oil
¼ teaspoon ground ginger
¼ teaspoon red pepper flakes
¼ teaspoon black pepper
4 cups white rice, cooked
2 green onions, sliced (optional)
½ tablespoon sesame seeds (optional)

1. Add the ground beef and minced garlic to a large skillet over medium heat.
2. Cook, breaking up the beef, for 7 to 9 minutes or until the beef is fully cooked and no longer pink. Drain any excess grease, if needed.
3. While the beef is cooking, place the cucumber slices in a small bowl and stir to coat all slices. Set aside.
4. Whisk together the soy sauce, light brown sugar, toasted sesame oil, ground ginger, red pepper flakes, and black pepper in a small mixing bowl. Pour this mixture into the skillet with the cooked beef and stir to combine.
5. Cook for an additional 5 minutes, allowing the flavors to meld.
6. Divide the cooked rice among four serving bowls (1 cup per bowl).
7. Top each with the beef mixture. If using, garnish with sliced green onions and sesame seeds. Add the vinegar-marinated cucumber slices to each bowl. Serve immediately.

WATCHING YOUR SODIUM?

* Use a low-sodium soy sauce.

GLUTEN FREE?

* Make sure your soy sauce is too.

LIKE SPICE?

* Add ½ - 1 tablespoon of Sriracha sauce to the mixing bowl in step 3.

TYPES OF RICE:

* If you're using rice that takes longer to cook than instant rice, cook it first to ensure it's ready when the beef is done.

Hearty Beef Chili

This robust dish combines ground beef, hearty beans, and vibrant vegetables simmered in a rich, flavorful tomato sauce, perfect for an easy, yet cozy meal. This freezes well for emergency meals or a freezer meal prep.

SERVES: 6-8 **PREP:** 10 MINUTES **COOK:** 35 MINUTES **TOTAL:** 45 MINUTES

1 tablespoon avocado oil (or olive oil)
1 pound lean ground beef
1 yellow onion, diced
2 celery stalks, diced
1 red pepper, diced
1 green pepper, diced
4 cloves garlic, minced
1 teaspoon salt
¼ teaspoon black pepper
1 (28 oz) can crushed tomatoes
1 (14 oz/398 ml) can fire-roasted tomatoes
1 (14 oz/398 ml) can brown sugar baked beans
1 (14 oz/398 ml) can red kidney beans, drained and rinsed
1 cup beef broth
2 tablespoons tomato paste
2 tablespoons chili powder
2 teaspoons cumin
1 teaspoon brown sugar
1 teaspoon red wine vinegar

Optional Toppings:
Tortilla chips, crushed
Greek yogurt or sour cream
Shredded cheddar or Tex-Mex cheese
Green onions

1. Heat the avocado oil in a large pot over medium heat. Add the ground beef, onion, celery, red pepper, green pepper, garlic, salt, and black pepper. Cook until the beef is no longer pink and the onions are translucent, about 5 minutes.
2. Stir in the crushed tomatoes, fire-roasted tomatoes, baked beans, red kidney beans, beef broth, tomato paste, chili powder, cumin, brown sugar, and red wine vinegar. Bring the mixture to a boil.
3. Reduce the heat to low and let the chili simmer, uncovered, for 30 minutes, stirring often.
4. Serve the chili as is or top with optional toppings such as crushed tortilla chips, Greek yogurt or sour cream, shredded cheese, or green onions.

LEFTOVER IDEAS

* Leftovers can be used in other dishes like a Loaded Chili Baked Potato (Page 25).

PREP TIP

* Dice the vegetables to a uniform size to ensure even cooking.

Loaded Chili Baked Potato

This satisfying dish features a baked russet potato loaded with hearty chili, melted cheese, and a dollop of creamy Greek yogurt or sour cream, topped with fresh chives or green onions.

SERVES: 4 **PREP:** 1 MINUTE **COOK:** 55 MINUTES **TOTAL:** 56 MINUTES

4 russet potatoes
2 cups chili (use leftover hearty beef chili or any chili on hand)
1 cup shredded cheddar cheese
¼ cup Greek yogurt or sour cream
¼ cup chopped chives or green onions

Topping Ideas:
Sliced jalapeños
Diced tomatoes
Crumbled bacon

1. Cook the Potatoes:

   Oven Instructions: Preheat the oven to 450°F (232°C). Poke each potato with a fork 4-5 times. Place the potatoes directly on the oven rack and bake for 45 minutes or until the potatoes are soft and easily pierced with a fork.

   Microwave Instructions: Poke each potato with a fork 4-5 times. Microwave on high for 4-5 minutes. Check the potatoes; if not fully cooked, flip them over and microwave for another 4-5 minutes. For multiple potatoes, add 1 minute per additional potato, but don't cook more than 4 potatoes at a time.
2. Slice each baked potato open and fluff the insides with a fork. Add ½ cup of chili to each potato.
3. Top each potato with shredded cheese. If using the oven, return the potatoes to the oven and bake for 10 minutes at 450°F (232°C). For until the cheese is melted. If using the microwave, heat for 1-2 minutes in 30-second intervals until the cheese is melted.
4. Top with Greek yogurt or sour cream, and sprinkle with chives or green onions. Serve hot.

RECIPE TIPS

* Adjust the amount of chili and cheese based on your preference.
* If you're short on time, the microwave method is faster, but the oven method gives a crispier skin.
* Fluffing the insides of the potato before adding toppings helps to distribute the flavors better.

One-Pan Ground Beef Stroganoff

This hearty and creamy dinner combines savory beef, tender noodles, and a rich mushroom sauce for a quick and comforting meal ready in just 30 minutes.

SERVES: 6 **PREP:** 5 MINUTES **COOK:** 25 MINUTES **TOTAL:** 30 MINUTES

1 pound lean ground beef
1 sweet onion, chopped
1 cup cremini mushrooms, sliced
1 tablespoon Worcestershire sauce
¼ cup all-purpose flour
5 cups beef broth
4 cups extra wide egg noodles, uncooked
1 teaspoon Dijon mustard
1 teaspoon salt
½ teaspoon dried thyme or 1 tablespoon fresh thyme
¼ teaspoon black pepper
⅔ cup sour cream

1. In a large deep fry pan, cook the ground beef, chopped onion, and sliced mushrooms over medium heat for 7 to 10 minutes, stirring frequently, until the beef is no longer pink and the vegetables are softened.
2. Stir in the Worcestershire sauce to combine.
3. Sprinkle the all-purpose flour over the mixture and stir constantly for 1 minute to incorporate.
4. Stir in the beef broth, uncooked egg noodles, Dijon mustard, salt, pepper, and thyme. Bring the mixture to a boil.
5. Reduce the heat to medium-low. Cover and simmer for 10 minutes, or until the egg noodles are cooked, stirring once or twice during the cooking process.
6. Remove the lid and stir in the sour cream until well combined. Heat for an additional 1 to 2 minutes. Serve hot.

SUBSTITUTIONS

* I used a 227g (8 oz) package of sliced cremini mushrooms but sliced white button mushrooms would also work.
* Wide egg noodles were used, but a smaller variety will also work.

GLUTEN FREE?

* Use a gluten-free egg noodle, and a gluten-free worcestershire sauce. Replace the all-purpose flour with brown rice flour.

RECIPE TIPS

* Use a large fry pan with a lid to prevent the liquid from overflowing when you add the beef broth.
* After cooking the ground beef, you don't need to drain the grease; the flour will absorb it and help thicken the sauce.

Muffin Tin Meatloaf

These savory meatloaf muffins, topped with a tangy glaze, offer a quick and easy meal that's both comforting and delicious.

MAKES: 18 **PREP:** 10 MINUTES **COOK:** 30 MINUTES **TOTAL:** 40 MINUTES

2 pounds lean ground beef
1 cup panko breadcrumbs
½ cup ketchup
2 tablespoons dried minced onions
1 tablespoon Worcestershire sauce
1 large egg
2 cloves garlic, minced
½ teaspoon salt
¼ teaspoon black pepper

Glaze:
½ cup ketchup
½ cup BBQ sauce
1 tablespoon light brown sugar
1 teaspoon onion powder

1. Preheat the oven to 350°F (175°C).
2. In a large bowl, combine the ground beef, panko breadcrumbs, ½ cup ketchup, minced onions, Worcestershire sauce, egg, garlic, salt, and pepper. Mix together with clean hands until all ingredients are well combined.
3. Divide the meat mixture evenly into a muffin pan by rolling the meat into balls about 2 inches in diameter and placing them in each muffin well. Slightly flatten the top of each muffin with clean fingers or the back of a spoon. This recipe makes about 18 meatloaf muffins, so you may need two muffin pans.
4. In a small mixing bowl, combine ½ cup ketchup, BBQ sauce, brown sugar, and onion powder. Stir to combine.
5. Add about 1 tablespoon of glaze on top of each meatloaf muffin.
6. Bake for 30 minutes or until the internal temperature of the meatloaf muffins reaches 160°F (71°C). Serve hot.

SUBSTITUTIONS

* Dried minced onions can be found in the spice aisle at the grocery store. If you can't find dried minced onions, use 2 tablespoons of onion flakes or 1 teaspoon onion powder.

TIPS

* You don't need to grease the muffin pan as the meatloaf will release enough fat to prevent sticking.
* Use a garlic press to mince the garlic if you have one.
* It's much easier to use your hands to mix the meat mixture. Just make sure your hands are clean and wash them well afterward.
* Serve with mashed potatoes and steamed vegetables for a complete meal.

Salisbury Steak with Mushroom Gravy

This comforting dish features juicy beef patties smothered in a rich mushroom gravy, perfect for serving over mashed potatoes or rice.

SERVES: 6 **PREP:** 10 MINUTES **COOK:** 23 MINUTES **TOTAL:** 33 MINUTES

Salisbury Steak:

1 pound lean ground beef
¾ cup Panko breadcrumbs
¼ cup ketchup
1 large egg
1 tablespoon dried minced onion
1 tablespoon Dijon mustard
1 teaspoon Worcestershire sauce
1 teaspoon salt
½ teaspoon garlic powder
¼ teaspoon black pepper
2 tablespoons salted butter

Mushroom Gravy:

1 sweet onion, diced
1 cup cremini mushrooms, sliced
4 tablespoons all-purpose flour
2 cups beef broth
1 tablespoon tomato paste
1 teaspoon Worcestershire sauce
½ teaspoon salt
¼ teaspoon black pepper

1. In a large bowl, combine the ground beef, Panko breadcrumbs, ketchup, egg, dried minced onion, Dijon mustard, Worcestershire sauce, salt, garlic powder, and black pepper. Mix together with clean hands until well combined. Shape the meat mixture into 6 oval-shaped patties about ¾ inch thick.
2. Melt butter in a large skillet over medium heat. Add the patties to the skillet and cook for 6 minutes per side or until the meat is no longer pink. Remove the cooked patties to a plate and set aside.
3. In the same skillet, add the diced sweet onions and sliced mushrooms. Cook over medium heat until the onions are softened, about 5 minutes. Add the flour to the skillet and cook, stirring constantly, for 1 minute. Gradually stir in the beef broth, tomato paste, Worcestershire sauce, salt, and pepper. Continue stirring until the mixture thickens, about 1 to 2 minutes.
4. Return the patties to the skillet, spooning the gravy over them to cover. Cook for an additional 2 to 3 minutes until heated through. Serve hot.

SUBSTITUTIONS

* White button mushrooms can be substitute cremini.
* No dried minced onion? Substitute with 1 teaspoon of onion powder.

RECIPE TIPS

* Don't drain the grease after cooking the patties; it will be used to cook the mushrooms and onions.
* Avoid making the patties too thick to ensure they cook through.
* Mixing the ground beef mixture with your hands is much easier than using a spoon.
* Ground beef should be cooked to an internal temperature of 160°F (71°C).

Philly Cheesesteak Sloppy Joes

Ground beef, melted cheese, and tangy sauce come together on toasted buns for a quick and easy dinner the whole family will enjoy.

MAKES: 6 **PREP:** 5 MINUTES **COOK:** 15 MINUTES **TOTAL:** 20 MINUTES

6 hamburger buns
1 pound lean ground beef
1 sweet onion, diced
1 green pepper, diced
3 cloves garlic, minced
2 tablespoons Worcestershire sauce
2 tablespoons all-purpose flour
1 cup beef broth
2 tablespoons ketchup
1 teaspoon Dijon mustard
½ teaspoon paprika
½ teaspoon salt
¼ teaspoon black pepper
2 cups white cheddar cheese, shredded

1. Preheat the oven to 350°F (175°C). Lay out both sides of the hamburger buns on a baking sheet in a single layer. Depending on the size of your buns and baking sheet, you may need to use two baking sheets. Bake for 5 minutes. Set aside.
2. Add the ground beef, diced onion, diced green pepper, and minced garlic to a large skillet over medium heat. Cook for 7 to 10 minutes until the beef is no longer pink and the vegetables are softened. Stir in the Worcestershire sauce.
3. Sprinkle the flour over the beef mixture and continue cooking for 1 minute, stirring constantly to incorporate the flour.
4. Stir in the beef broth, ketchup, Dijon mustard, paprika, salt, and black pepper. Cook over medium heat, stirring frequently, for 5 minutes until the mixture thickens.
5. Remove the skillet from the heat and mix in the shredded white cheddar cheese until melted and well combined.
6. Serve the meat mixture on the toasted hamburger buns

PREP TIPS

* Use a garlic press to mince the garlic if you have one for convenience and efficiency.

TIPS

* After the ground beef is cooked, you don't need to drain the grease from the pan; the flour will absorb it and help thicken the sauce.
* If you can't find white cheddar, you can substitute Monterey Jack or mozzarella cheese.

Beef Burrito Bowls

This flavorful and hearty dinner combines seasoned ground beef, fresh vegetables, and zesty toppings over a bed of rice for a satisfying meal in just 35 minutes.

SERVES: 6 **PREP:** 10 MINUTES **COOK:** 25 MINUTES **TOTAL:** 35 MINUTES

1 pound lean ground beef
1 sweet onion, chopped
1 red pepper, chopped
1 packet (3 tablespoons) taco seasoning
1 can (15 oz) black beans, drained and rinsed
1 ½ cups corn (fresh, canned, or frozen)
1 can (4 oz) green chilies
3 tomatoes, chopped
1 teaspoon salt
¼ teaspoon black pepper
½ cup taco sauce
½ cup sour cream
1 teaspoon lime juice
3 cups cooked white rice

Topping Ideas:
Shredded cheddar cheese
Guacamole
Salsa
Refried beans

1. Add the ground beef, chopped onion, and red pepper to a large skillet over medium heat. Cook, stirring often to break up the beef, for 7 to 10 minutes, until the beef is cooked and the vegetables are softened. Stir in the taco seasoning.
2. Stir in the black beans, corn, green chilies, chopped tomatoes, salt, and black pepper. Continue to cook over medium heat for 15 minutes, stirring occasionally.
3. In a small bowl, stir together the taco sauce, sour cream, and lime juice. Set aside.
4. Add the cooked rice to the beef mixture and stir to combine.
5. Divide the beef and rice mixture into serving bowls. Top with the taco sauce/sour cream mixture and any additional toppings you use.

PREP TIPS

* Start preparing the rice according to package directions when preparing the beef.
* You can cook the rice ahead of time if you wish. If the rice is not hot when you add it to the beef mixture, heat it for 3 to 4 minutes before serving.

RECIPE TIPS

* Add a squeeze of fresh lime juice and a sprinkle of chopped cilantro to each bowl for extra flavor.
* Serve with tortilla chips for added crunch.

Ginger Beef Stir Fry

Tender steak strips, crisp vegetables, and a savory ginger sauce make this quick recipe a perfect pick for busy weeknights.

MAKES: 4 **PREP:** 15 MINUTES **COOK:** 15 MINUTES **TOTAL:** 30 MINUTES

¼ cup peanut oil
1 pound sirloin steak or sirloin tip steak, sliced into 1-inch strips
1 head of broccoli, cut into florets
3 baby bok choy, roughly chopped
2 celery stalks, chopped
1 red pepper, sliced into 1-inch strips
1 green pepper, sliced into 1-inch strips
1 tablespoon minced ginger
3 cloves garlic, minced
3 green onions, sliced

Ginger Sauce:

5 tablespoons soy sauce
2 tablespoons rice vinegar
2 tablespoons cornstarch
2 tablespoons hoisin sauce
1 tablespoon minced ginger
1 tablespoon honey
½ teaspoon salt

1. Heat the peanut oil in a large skillet or wok over medium heat. Add the sliced steak, broccoli florets, baby bok choy, chopped celery, red pepper strips, green pepper strips, minced ginger, minced garlic, and sliced green onions. Cook for 10 minutes or until the steak is cooked and the vegetables are softened.
2. In a medium bowl, whisk together the soy sauce, rice vinegar, cornstarch, hoisin sauce, minced ginger, honey, and salt.
3. Pour the ginger sauce into the skillet or wok, stirring to combine. Cook for 3 to 5 minutes, stirring frequently, until the sauce thickens.
4. Serve hot on its own or over a bed of white rice.

SUBSTITUTIONS

* A high heat stable oil (avocado oil, coconut oil, canola oil) can be substituted for peanut oil.
* Regular bok choy can be used if you can't find baby bok choy. Use 2 cups of roughly chopped bok choy in its place.

TIPS

* Buy minced ginger in the produce section to save time. If unavailable, you can mince a thumb-sized piece of fresh ginger instead.
* Use a large skillet or wok, as this recipe has many ingredients, but they will shrink as they cook.

Sheet Pan Dinners

If you're looking for meals that are big on flavor but light on cleanup, you will love these!

Sheet pan dinners are a busy cook's best friend—just toss everything on a pan, pop it in the oven, and let it do the work for you. Whether you're craving something savory, sweet, or a little bit of both, these recipes have you covered.

Kick things off with the **Sheet Pan Steak Fajitas** *(41)* or **Sheet Pan Beef and Broccoli** *(42)* for a quick and satisfying dinner that's sure to please. For seafood lovers, the **Maple Salmon Sheet Pan Dinner** *(48)* and **Sheet Pan Old Bay® Shrimp and Sausage** *(52)* offer deliciously simple options that don't skimp on flavor.

If chicken is more your style, you'll love the **Sheet Pan Teriyaki Chicken and Pineapple** *(45)* or the **Honey Lemon Chicken Sheet Pan Dinner** *(46)*—both are perfect for a flavorful meal with minimal fuss. And for a comforting, all-in-one dish, the **Sheet Pan Parmesan Crusted Chicken and Broccoli with Potatoes** *(51)* is sure to become a new favorite.

These recipes are all about making dinner easy, delicious, and stress-free. So grab a sheet pan, gather your ingredients, and let's make dinner simple and satisfying!

Sheet Pan Steak Fajitas

Mouthwatering steak strips and colorful bell peppers roast together on one pan for a quick, flavorful dinner with easy clean-up

SERVES: 4 **PREP:** 10 MINUTES **COOK:** 18 MINUTES **TOTAL:** 28 MINUTES

1 to 1 ½ pound top sirloin steak, cut into strips
1 sweet onion, sliced
1 green pepper, cut into strips
1 red pepper, cut into strips
1 yellow pepper, cut into strips
3 tablespoons extra virgin olive oil
1 tablespoon lime juice
1 tablespoon chili powder
1 teaspoon cumin
1 teaspoon salt
½ teaspoon garlic powder
¼ teaspoon black pepper

1. Preheat the oven to 400°F (200°C). Line a large baking sheet with aluminum foil and spray with cooking spray.
2. In a large bowl, combine the sliced onions, green pepper, red pepper, yellow pepper, and steak strips.
3. In a small bowl, whisk together the extra virgin olive oil, lime juice, chili powder, cumin, salt, garlic powder, and black pepper. Pour the mixture over the steak and vegetables, tossing to ensure everything is evenly coated.
4. Spread the steak and vegetables in a single layer on the prepared baking sheet. Bake for 16 to 18 minutes until the steak is cooked to your desired doneness and the vegetables are tender.
5. Serve with tortillas and your favorite fajita toppings such as salsa, sour cream, cheddar cheese, and guacamole.

NOTE:

* I used two top sirloin steaks, which weighed a little over 1 pound. You can also use other cuts of steak, such as round, skirt, or flank steak.

TIPS

* For added flavor, let the steak and vegetables marinate in the olive oil and spice mixture for 15-30 minutes before baking.
* Cooking time may vary depending on the thickness of your steak. Keep an eye on it during the last few minutes of cooking to ensure the steak is done to your liking.

Sheet Pan Beef and Broccoli

This quick and easy one-pan dinner combines tender beef strips and broccoli, all baked in a savory soy-garlic sauce, for a delicious and effortless meal.

SERVES: 4 **PREP:** 5 MINUTES **COOK:** 20 MINUTES **TOTAL:** 25 MINUTES

½ pound striploin steak (about 2 to 3 steaks), sliced into 1-inch long strips
1 head of broccoli, chopped into florets
¼ cup soy sauce
2 tablespoons brown sugar
1 tablespoon toasted sesame oil
2 teaspoons rice vinegar
3 cloves garlic, minced
2 green onions, sliced
¼ teaspoon black pepper
½ tablespoon sesame seeds (optional)

1. Preheat the oven to 425°F (220°C). Line a baking sheet with aluminum foil and spray with cooking spray.
2. Add the sliced steak and broccoli florets to a large bowl.
3. In a small bowl, whisk together the soy sauce, brown sugar, toasted sesame oil, rice vinegar, minced garlic, green onions, and black pepper. Pour the mixture over the steak and broccoli, tossing to combine and ensure everything is evenly coated.
4. Spread the steak and broccoli mixture in a single layer on the prepared baking sheet. Bake for 20 minutes or until the steak is cooked to your desired doneness and the broccoli is tender.
5. Sprinkle with sesame seeds, if desired, and serve hot.

NOTES

* If you want to reduce the saltiness, use reduced-sodium soy sauce.
* You can substitute other cuts of beef for the striploin, such as sirloin, flank, or round steak.
* For added flavor, marinate the steak and broccoli in the soy sauce mixture for 15-30 minutes before baking.

TIPS

* Serve over rice or noodles for a complete meal.
* Save time by using pre-cut broccoli.

Sheet Pan Teriyaki Chicken and Pineapple

Bite-sized chicken, fresh vegetables, and pineapple coated in a sweet and tangy teriyaki glaze roast together on one pan for an easy, flavorful meal.

SERVES: 4 **PREP:** 10 MINUTES **COOK:** 25 MINUTES **TOTAL:** 35 MINUTES

4 boneless, skinless chicken breasts cut into bite-sized pieces (about 1 inch)
2 red peppers, cut into strips
1 red onion, sliced
2 cups fresh pineapple chunks
¾ cup teriyaki sauce
2 tablespoons honey
2 tablespoons extra virgin olive oil
1 tablespoon chili garlic sauce
2 cloves garlic, minced
½ teaspoon salt
¼ teaspoon black pepper

1. Preheat the oven to 425°F (220°C). Line a baking sheet with aluminum foil and spray with cooking spray.
2. In a large bowl, combine the chicken, red peppers, red onion, and pineapple chunks.
3. In a small bowl, whisk together the teriyaki sauce, honey, extra virgin olive oil, chili garlic sauce, minced garlic, salt, and black pepper.
4. Pour the sauce mixture over the chicken and vegetables, tossing to ensure everything is evenly coated.
5. Spread the chicken and vegetable mixture in a single layer on the prepared baking sheet. Bake for 25 minutes or until the chicken is fully cooked and the vegetables are tender. Serve hot.

NOTE:

* I used pre-cut pineapple chunks from the produce section. If fresh pineapple isn't available, you can also use canned pineapple chunks (drain the juice).

TIPS

* This dish is delicious served on a bed of rice.
* Look for the teriyaki sauce and chili garlic sauce in the Asian section of the grocery store, usually near the soy sauce.
* Use a garlic press to mince the garlic if you have one for convenience.

Honey Lemon Chicken Sheet Pan Dinner

This vibrant sheet pan meal features tender chicken, crisp asparagus, and roasted potatoes all coated in a tangy honey lemon glaze.

SERVES: 4 **PREP:** 10 MINUTES **COOK:** 30 MINUTES **TOTAL:** 40 MINUTES

4 boneless, skinless chicken breasts, cut into 1-inch pieces
1 bunch of asparagus (about 1 pound), trimmed
1 ½ pound yellow mini potatoes, cut into quarters
⅓ cup lemon juice
¼ cup honey
1 tablespoon soy sauce
1 tablespoon extra virgin olive oil
3 garlic cloves, minced
1 teaspoon dried rosemary
½ teaspoon paprika
½ teaspoon onion powder
½ teaspoon salt
¼ teaspoon black pepper

1. Preheat the oven to 400°F (200°C). Line a large baking sheet with aluminum foil and spray with cooking spray.
2. In a large bowl, combine the chicken breast pieces, asparagus, and mini potatoes.
3. In a small bowl, whisk together the lemon juice, honey, soy sauce, extra virgin olive oil, minced garlic, dried rosemary, paprika, onion powder, salt, and black pepper.
4. Pour the lemon juice mixture over the chicken, asparagus, and potatoes. Toss to ensure everything is evenly coated.
5. Spread the mixture in a single, even layer on the prepared baking sheet. Bake for 30 minutes until the chicken is cooked to an internal temperature of 165°F (74°C) and the potatoes are tender. Serve hot.

NOTES

* You can substitute other potatoes, including red mini potatoes or baking potatoes. Just make sure they are chopped into small (½-inch) cubes, so they bake completely.
* You may use fresh or bottled lemon juice for this recipe.

TIPS

* Use a meat thermometer to check the internal temperature of the chicken to ensure it's fully cooked (165°F for chicken).

Maple Salmon Sheet Pan Dinner

This delicious, easy sheet pan dinner features tender salmon fillets and roasted vegetables coated with a sweet, tangy maple mustard glaze.

SERVES: 4 **PREP:** 10 MINUTES **COOK:** 32 MINUTES **TOTAL:** 42 MINUTES

1 sweet potato, peeled and chopped into ½-inch cubes
1 head of broccoli, cut into florets
1 sweet onion, sliced
5 tablespoons extra virgin olive oil, divided
1 teaspoon salt, divided
½ teaspoon black pepper, divided
¼ cup maple syrup
2 tablespoons wholegrain mustard
1 tablespoon lemon juice
1 teaspoon paprika
1 teaspoon dried thyme
4 salmon filets (4 to 6 oz each)

1. Preheat the oven to 425°F (220°C). Line a large baking sheet with aluminum foil and spray with cooking spray.
2. In a large bowl, combine the sweet potatoes, broccoli, and onion. Add 3 tablespoons of extra virgin olive oil, ½ teaspoon salt, and ¼ teaspoon black pepper. Toss until well combined. Spread the vegetables in a single layer on the prepared baking sheet and roast for 15 minutes.
3. While the vegetables are roasting, in a small bowl, whisk together the maple syrup, wholegrain mustard, lemon juice, paprika, thyme, 2 tablespoons of extra virgin olive oil, ½ teaspoon salt, and ¼ teaspoon black pepper.
4. After 15 minutes, remove the baking sheet from the oven. Move the vegetables to the sides of the pan to make room for the salmon filets. Place the salmon filets in the center of the baking sheet. Brush the maple syrup mixture onto each salmon filet. Spread any leftover glaze over the vegetables.
5. Return the baking sheet to the oven and bake for another 15 to 17 minutes, depending on the thickness of your salmon filets, until the salmon is cooked through and flakes easily with a fork. Serve hot.

NOTES

* Wholegrain mustard offers excellent texture and flavor, but Dijon mustard can be used as a substitute.

TIPS

* Use aluminum foil lined with cooking spray to prevent sticking and make cleanup easier.
* Ensure the sweet potatoes are cut into small, even pieces to ensure they cook through.
* Large salmon filets can be cut in half to create four portions.

Parmesan Crusted Chicken & Broccoli with Potatoes

Crispy Parmesan-crusted chicken, tender broccoli, and roasted potatoes come together on one pan for an easy, flavorful meal.

SERVES: 4 **PREP:** 10 MINUTES **COOK:** 30 MINUTES **TOTAL:** 40 MINUTES

1 head of broccoli, chopped into florets
½ pound yellow mini potatoes (about 15 to 20), chopped into ½-inch cubes
¼ cup extra virgin olive oil
1 teaspoon salt, divided
½ teaspoon black pepper, divided
1 cup Panko breadcrumbs
½ cup grated Parmesan cheese
1 teaspoon Italian seasoning
½ teaspoon garlic powder
½ teaspoon onion powder
1 large egg
1 tablespoon water
4 boneless, skinless chicken breasts

1. Preheat the oven to 425°F (220°C). Line a baking sheet with aluminum foil and spray with cooking spray.
2. In a large bowl, combine the broccoli florets and mini potatoes. Add the extra virgin olive oil, ½ teaspoon of salt, and ¼ teaspoon of black pepper. Toss to combine and spread the mixture evenly on the prepared baking sheet.
3. In a small bowl, mix the panko breadcrumbs, grated Parmesan cheese, Italian seasoning, garlic powder, onion powder, ½ teaspoon of salt, and ¼ teaspoon of black pepper.
4. In another small bowl, whisk together the egg and water.
5. Dip each chicken breast into the egg mixture, ensuring it is fully covered, then dip into the breadcrumb mixture, pressing to coat evenly. Place the coated chicken breasts on the baking sheet, making room by pushing the broccoli and potatoes to the sides if necessary.
6. Bake for 30 minutes until the chicken is cooked and the potatoes are tender. Serve hot.

NOTE:

* You can substitute other types of potatoes, such as red mini potatoes or baking potatoes. Ensure they are chopped into small (½-inch) cubes to bake completely.
* You may need to push the broccoli and potatoes to the sides to make room for the chicken breasts on the baking sheet.

TIPS

* Use a meat thermometer to check the internal temperature of the chicken to ensure it's fully cooked (165°F).

Sheet Pan OLD BAY® Shrimp & Sausage

Succulent shrimp, savory sausage, and fresh vegetables, all seasoned with OLD BAY®, roast together on one pan for a delicious and easy dinner.

SERVES: 4 **PREP:** 10 MINUTES **COOK:** 30 MINUTES **TOTAL:** 40 MINUTES

1 pound raw large shrimp, peeled and deveined
4 mild Italian sausages, cut into 1-inch pieces
½ pound red mini potatoes, chopped into ½-inch cubes
3 shallots, peeled and cut into wedges
1 bunch asparagus (about 1 pound), trimmed
¼ cup extra virgin olive oil
2 tablespoons lemon juice
1 tablespoon OLD BAY® Seasoning
½ teaspoon salt
¼ teaspoon black pepper

1. Preheat the oven to 400°F (200°C). Line a baking sheet with aluminum foil and spray with cooking spray.
2. In a large bowl, combine the sausage, mini potatoes, shallots, and asparagus.
3. In a medium bowl, add the shrimp.
4. In a small bowl, whisk together the extra virgin olive oil, lemon juice, OLD BAY® Seasoning, salt, and black pepper.
5. Add 1 tablespoon of the seasoning mixture to the shrimp and toss to combine.
6. Pour the remaining seasoning mixture over the sausage and vegetable mixture and toss to combine.
7. Spread the sausage and vegetable mixture in a single layer on the prepared baking sheet. Bake for 20 minutes.
8. After 20 minutes, add the seasoned shrimp to the baking sheet. Bake for an additional 10 minutes, or until the shrimp are cooked through and the vegetables are tender. Serve hot.

NOTES

* You can substitute other types of potatoes, such as red mini potatoes or baking potatoes. Ensure they are chopped into small (½-inch) cubes to bake completely.
* Frozen raw shrimp (1 pound/600g) packages work well, but make sure to thaw the shrimp before using. This typically equals about 31 to 40 shrimp.
* If you can't find shallots, use ½ a red onion, peeled and sliced.
* For a spicier dish, use hot Italian sausage or chorizo sausage.

TIPS

* Remove the tails from the shrimp, if desired, for easier eating.
* Save time by using pre-cut broccoli.

Fish & Seafood

If you're looking to add a little coastal flair to your busy weeknights, you're in for a treat. This chapter is filled with light, flavorful dishes that are quick to prepare but still pack a punch in the taste department.

Start with the classic **Shrimp Scampi with Linguine** *(57)* for a dish that feels fancy but comes together in no time. If you're in the mood for something tropical, the **Baked Pineapple Salmon** *(58)* offers a sweet and savory twist that's sure to brighten up your dinner table.

For a quick, zesty option, try the **Sweet and Sour Glazed Shrimp** *(61)*—it's perfect for those nights when you want bold flavors without a lot of effort. The **Teriyaki Salmon with Broccoli** *(62)* is another easy choice that brings together tender fish and fresh veggies in a delicious, sticky sauce.

For a simple yet satisfying meal, the **Salmon in Foil with Veggies** *(65)* and **Garlic Lemon Baked Tilapia** *(66)* are perfect go-tos. They're both light, healthy, and require minimal cleanup, making them ideal for busy evenings.

And for a fun twist on a classic, don't miss the **Crab Cake Burgers** *(69)*—they're a tasty, handheld option that's sure to become a new family favorite.

These recipes are all about making seafood approachable and delicious, even on the busiest of days. So dive in, and let's bring a little bit of the ocean to your dinner table!

Shrimp Scampi with Linguine

Tender shrimp sautéed in buttery garlic sauce, tossed with linguine, and finished with lemon and Parmesan create a quick, mouthwatering dish.

SERVES: 4 **PREP:** 5 MINUTES **COOK:** 10 MINUTES **TOTAL:** 15 MINUTES

3 tablespoons salted butter
1 to 1 ½ pounds raw large shrimp, peeled and deveined
4 garlic cloves, minced
¼ cup lemon juice
¼ cup chicken broth
1 teaspoon salt
½ teaspoon dried oregano
¼ teaspoon black pepper
8 oz linguine, cooked (Use ½ package of pasta)
¼ cup Parmesan cheese, grated

1. Melt the butter in a large skillet over medium heat. Add the shrimp and garlic and sauté for 2 minutes, stirring often until the shrimp start to turn pink.
2. Stir in the lemon juice, chicken broth, salt, dried oregano, and black pepper. Cook for an additional 5 minutes on medium heat, stirring frequently until the shrimp are fully cooked and the sauce is slightly reduced.
3. Add the cooked linguine and Parmesan cheese to the skillet. Toss to coat the pasta evenly with the sauce. Serve hot.

NOTES

* If you're watching your sodium intake, you can use unsalted butter.
* You can use either fresh lemon juice or bottled lemon juice.

RECIPE TIPS

* Remove the tails from the shrimp, if desired, for easier eating.
* If preferred, you can use frozen shrimp. Thaw in the fridge for 24 hours or in a colander under cold running water for a few minutes.
* Start cooking the linguine first as it will take the longest to cook.

Baked Pineapple Salmon

This dinner recipe features tender salmon baked with sweet chili sauce, honey, and garlic, served atop juicy pineapple slices for a delightful blend of flavors.

SERVES: 6 **PREP:** 5 MINUTES **COOK:** 30 MINUTES **TOTAL:** 35 MINUTES

5 slices of pineapple
2 ½ to 3 pound large salmon filet
¼ cup sweet chili sauce
2 tablespoons honey
2 tablespoons extra virgin olive oil
2 tablespoons lemon juice
3 cloves garlic, minced
½ teaspoon salt
¼ teaspoon black pepper

1. Preheat the oven to 400°F (200°C). Line a baking sheet with aluminum foil and spray with cooking spray.
2. Lay pineapple slices in the center of the baking sheet lengthwise. Place the salmon filet on top of the pineapple slices.
3. In a small bowl, whisk together the sweet chili sauce, honey, extra virgin olive oil, lemon juice, minced garlic, salt, and black pepper. Spoon the mixture evenly over the salmon filet.
4. Bake for 30 minutes, or until the salmon is cooked through. The internal temperature should reach between 145°F to 160°F (63°C to 71°C). Cut into pieces and serve hot.

NOTES

* I used 1 can of pineapple slices. You may have extra slices.
* Sweet chili sauce can be found in the Asian food section of the grocery store.
* Use either bottled lemon juice or fresh lemon juice.
* Baking time may vary depending on the thickness of the salmon and your oven. I highly recommend using a meat thermometer to check for doneness.

TIPS

* Serve with a side of steamed rice or a fresh green salad to complete the meal.

Sweet and Sour Glazed Shrimp

Juicy shrimp sautéed with green onions and ginger, then glazed in a tangy sweet and sour sauce, deliver a quick and flavorful meal.

SERVES: 4 **PREP:** 5 MINUTES **COOK:** 8 MINUTES **TOTAL:** 13 MINUTES

1 pound small raw shrimp, peeled and deveined (61 to 70 shrimp)
½ teaspoon salt
¼ teaspoon black pepper
1 tablespoon toasted sesame oil
2 green onions, sliced
1 teaspoon fresh minced ginger
¼ cup rice vinegar
¼ cup brown sugar
¼ cup plum sauce
1 tablespoon lime juice
1 teaspoon cornstarch

1. Add the shrimp to a mixing bowl. Pat dry with a paper towel. Add the salt and black pepper and gently toss to combine.
2. Heat the toasted sesame oil in a large skillet over medium heat. Add the shrimp, green onions, and ginger. Cook for 3 minutes, stirring frequently.
3. In a small mixing bowl, whisk together the rice vinegar, brown sugar, plum sauce, lime juice, and cornstarch. Add the sauce to the skillet and stir to combine. Cook for an additional 3 minutes, or until the shrimp are cooked through and the sauce is slightly thickened.
4. Serve hot over cooked rice.

NOTE:

* You can use a package of large shrimp instead of small shrimp, if preferred.
* Use either freshly minced ginger or pre-minced ginger from a jar.
* To make the sauce thicker, add another teaspoon of cornstarch.

TIPS

* Remove the tails from the shrimp, if desired, for easier eating.
* You can use frozen shrimp; thaw it in the fridge for 24 hours or in a colander under cold running water for a few minutes.

Teriyaki Salmon with Broccoli

A fast and delicious dinner with salmon filets and a medley of vibrant vegetables coated in a savory teriyaki sauce..

SERVES: 4 **PREP:** 10 MINUTES **COOK:** 15 MINUTES **TOTAL:** 25 MINUTES

4 tablespoons extra virgin olive oil, divided
4 salmon filets (4 to 6 oz each)
1 head broccoli, cut into florets
1 red pepper, chopped
1 green pepper, chopped
1 sweet onion, chopped
2 teaspoons minced fresh ginger
3 cloves garlic, minced
¼ cup soy sauce
2 tablespoons honey
2 tablespoons rice vinegar
¼ teaspoon black pepper

1. Heat 2 tablespoons of extra virgin olive oil in a large skillet over medium heat. Add the broccoli, red pepper, green pepper, onion, ginger, and garlic. Cook for 11 to 13 minutes, stirring frequently, until the vegetables are tender.
2. Meanwhile, in another skillet, heat the remaining 2 tablespoons of extra virgin olive oil over medium heat. Add the salmon filets and cook for about 5 to 7 minutes per side, or until the salmon is cooked through and flakes easily with a fork.
3. In a small bowl, whisk together the soy sauce, honey, rice vinegar, and black pepper. Add the sauce to the vegetable mixture and cook for an additional 2 minutes, stirring to combine.
4. Add the cooked salmon filets to the vegetable mixture and spoon the sauce over the top. Serve hot, with rice, if desired.

NOTES

* I don't add extra salt because soy sauce is usually quite salty.
* Use a meat thermometer to check your salmon for doneness. It should be between 125°F and 145°F. Salmon cooking time may vary depending on the thickness of the filets.

TIPS

* To save time, use jarred minced ginger, typically found in the produce section at the grocery store.
* Serve with steamed rice or quinoa to make it a complete meal.

Salmon in Foil with Veggies

A simple and tasty dish with salmon and fresh vegetables, all cooked in foil packets with a zesty lemon-garlic sauce.

SERVES: 4 **PREP:** 10 MINUTES **COOK:** 30 MINUTES **TOTAL:** 40 MINUTES

4 salmon filets (4 to 6 oz each)
1 bunch of asparagus, trimmed (1 pound)
1 red pepper, sliced
1 sweet onion, sliced
1 cup grape tomatoes
¼ cup extra virgin olive oil
2 tablespoons lemon juice
1 tablespoon fresh thyme
3 garlic cloves, minced
½ teaspoon salt
¼ teaspoon black pepper

1. Preheat the oven to 400°F (200°C).
2. Lay out 4 squares of aluminum foil. Place 1 salmon filet in the center of each square. Arrange the asparagus, red pepper, onion, and grape tomatoes around and on top of the salmon filets.
3. In a small bowl, whisk together the extra virgin olive oil, lemon juice, fresh thyme, minced garlic, salt, and black pepper.
4. Spoon 2 tablespoons of the sauce mixture over each salmon filet and the surrounding veggies. Wrap up the foil packets, folding the edges to seal.
5. Place the foil packets on a baking sheet. Bake for 30 minutes until the salmon is cooked and the vegetables are softened. Serve hot.

NOTE:

* Cherry tomatoes can be used in place of grape tomatoes.
* You can use either bottled or fresh lemon juice.
* If you don't have fresh thyme, use ½ teaspoon of dried thyme.

TIPS

* Use a meat thermometer to check your salmon for doneness. It should be between 125°F and 145°F. Cooking time may vary depending on the thickness of the salmon filets.
* You can also cut a large salmon filet into four pieces.

Garlic Lemon Baked Tilapia

This quick and easy dinner features tender tilapia filets baked with a zesty lemon-garlic sauce for a light and flavorful meal.

SERVES: 4 | **PREP:** 5 MINUTES | **COOK:** 12 MINUTES | **TOTAL:** 17 MINUTES

3 to 4 tilapia filets, uncooked, boneless, skinless
¼ cup extra virgin olive oil
2 tablespoons lemon juice
4 garlic cloves, minced
½ teaspoon paprika
½ teaspoon salt
¼ teaspoon black pepper

1. Preheat the oven to 400°F (200°C).
2. Pat the tilapia filets dry with a paper towel and place them in a 9x13 inch casserole dish.
3. In a small bowl, whisk together the extra virgin olive oil, lemon juice, garlic, paprika, salt, and black pepper. Pour the mixture over the tilapia filets, ensuring they are well coated.
4. Bake for 10 to 12 minutes or until the tilapia is cooked and flakes easily with a fork. Serve hot.

NOTES

* You can use either bottled or fresh lemon juice.
* If using frozen tilapia filets, make sure they are thawed before cooking.

TIPS

* Serve with a side of steamed vegetables or a fresh salad to complete the meal.
* A meat thermometer can be used to check the tilapia for doneness. It should reach an internal temperature of 145°F (63°C).

Crab Cake Burgers

These flavorful burgers feature tender crab patties seasoned with OLD BAY® and topped with your favorite fixings for a delicious seafood twist on a classic sandwich.

SERVES: 4 **PREP:** 5 MINUTES **COOK:** 12 MINUTES **TOTAL:** 17 MINUTES

2 tablespoons extra virgin olive oil
1 pound crab meat
½ cup saltines, crushed
⅓ cup tartar sauce
¼ cup all-purpose flour
2 tablespoons fresh chives, chopped
1 tablespoon lemon juice
1 tablespoon Dijon mustard
1 large egg
2 teaspoons OLD BAY® Seasoning
¼ teaspoon black pepper
4 hamburger buns

Optional toppings:
Lettuce, sliced tomatoes, tartar sauce, mayonnaise, Dijon mustard, pickles

1. In a mixing bowl, combine the crab meat, crushed saltines, tartar sauce, all-purpose flour, fresh chives, lemon juice, Dijon mustard, egg, OLD BAY® Seasoning, and black pepper. Use clean hands to mix the ingredients until well combined.
2. Shape the crab mixture into 4 equal patties.
3. Heat the olive oil in a large skillet over medium-high heat. Add the crab patties to the skillet and cook for 5 minutes per side or until golden brown and cooked through.
4. Place each crab cake on a hamburger bun and top with your favorite toppings. Serve immediately.

NOTE:

* You can use bottled or fresh lemon juice.
* Saltines are also known as soda crackers.
* You can substitute with thinly sliced green onions if you don't have chives.
* Mayonnaise can be used instead of tartar sauce.
* Extra salt is not needed as OLD BAY® Seasoning contains salt.

TIPS

* Imitation crab is not recommended. Real crab meat, including canned crab meat, works best. I used 4 (120g) cans of chunk crab meat.
* Place the saltines in a plastic baggie and crush them with a rolling pin or your hands.
* If you have time, prepare the patties as directed and then chill them for 1 hour in the fridge. This will make it easier for them to flip with a spatula when cooking. Be gentle when flipping the crab cakes to prevent them from falling apart.

PASTA

If you're like us, pasta is your go-to comfort food, especially on those busy days when you need something quick, easy, and delicious. This chapter is all about celebrating the versatility of pasta with dishes that are sure to become weeknight staples in your home.

Craving something with a bit of a twist? The **One-Pot Enchilada Pasta** *(73)* brings the flavors of your favorite Mexican dish into a cozy, cheesy pasta meal that's perfect for a quick dinner. For a more classic comfort food experience, the **Spinach Artichoke Pasta** *(73)* offers a creamy, flavorful dish that's as satisfying as your favorite dip.

If you're in the mood for something fun and kid-friendly, the **Pizza Ravioli** *(77)* combines two favorites into one delicious, easy-to-make meal. For a little Southern flair, the **Cajun Orzo with Sausage** *(78)* adds a spicy kick that'll have you reaching for seconds.

The **Goulash** *(81)* is a hearty, comforting classic that's perfect for those nights when you want something filling and familiar. For a lighter option, the **Lemon Asparagus Chicken Pasta** *(82)* is a refreshing and zesty dish that feels like spring on a plate.

And if you're looking for something quick and flavorful, the **Sesame Garlic Ramen Noodles** *(85)* are a tasty, budget-friendly option that's ready in a flash.

These pasta recipes are all about making dinner delicious and stress-free, no matter how busy your day has been.

One-Pot Enchilada Pasta

This hearty one-pot dish combines ground beef, rotini noodles, black beans, and a zesty enchilada sauce, all topped with melted cheddar cheese and sour cream for a comforting and flavorful meal.

SERVES: 6 **PREP:** 10 MINUTES **COOK:** 30 MINUTES **TOTAL:** 40 MINUTES

1 pound lean ground beef
1 sweet onion, chopped
2 tablespoons taco seasoning
4 cups vegetable broth
4 cups rotini noodles, uncooked
3 (10 oz/284 ml) cans ROTEL® diced tomatoes with green chilies
1 (15 oz/540 ml) can black beans, drained and rinsed
1 (10 oz/296 ml) can red enchilada sauce
2 cups cheddar cheese, shredded
1 cup sour cream

1. Over medium heat, sauté the ground beef and chopped onion in a large pot or deep skillet. After about 4 minutes, stir in the taco seasoning. Cook for about 8 to 10 minutes, stirring frequently, until the beef is cooked and the onions softened.
2. Add the vegetable broth, rotini noodles, ROTEL® tomatoes, black beans, and enchilada sauce. Stir to combine. Bring to a boil, then reduce the heat to medium. Cook for 15 minutes, stirring often, or until the noodles are cooked.
3. Remove from heat and stir in the shredded cheddar cheese and sour cream. Serve hot.

NOTE:

* You can substitute beef broth for the vegetable broth.
* You can use another type of noodle such as rigatoni, penne, fusilli, or farfalle.
* Substitute 1 (28 oz) can of diced tomatoes if you can't find ROTEL®.
* If you can't find enchilada sauce, use 1 ¼ cups taco sauce or salsa. 1 packet of taco seasoning equals 2 tablespoons. Homemade taco seasoning works well too.
* Use mild or sharp cheddar cheese based on preference.

TIPS

* Ensure you use a pot that is large enough or a deep skillet, as you will need to add a significant amount of liquid initially.

Spinach Artichoke Pasta

This creamy pasta dish combines tender penne with savory spinach, artichokes, and a rich garlic-Parmesan sauce for a delightful and satisfying meal.

SERVES: 4 **PREP:** 5 MINUTES **COOK:** 15 MINUTES **TOTAL:** 20 MINUTES

4 cups penne, uncooked
¼ cup salted butter
4 cups baby spinach
4 cloves garlic, minced
¼ cup all-purpose flour
3 cups milk
½ teaspoon salt
¼ teaspoon black pepper
1 (8 oz/250 g) package of cream cheese, cut into 1-inch cubes
1 cup Parmesan cheese, grated
1 (14 oz/398 ml) can artichoke hearts, drained and roughly chopped

1. Cook the penne according to package directions. Drain and set aside.
2. Melt the butter in a large, deep skillet over medium heat. Add the baby spinach and garlic, cooking for 3 minutes while stirring often.
3. Add the all-purpose flour to the skillet and cook for 1 minute, stirring constantly.
4. Gradually add the milk, salt, and black pepper. Increase the heat to high and bring to a boil. Once boiling, reduce the heat to medium and cook for 5 minutes, stirring frequently until the mixture thickens.
5. Stir in the cream cheese, artichoke hearts, and Parmesan cheese. Continue stirring until the cream cheese is melted and the sauce is smooth, about 3 to 5 minutes.
6. Add the cooked penne to the sauce and stir until the pasta is evenly coated. Serve hot.

NOTES

* You can use other types of pasta like rigatoni, fusilli, or farfalle.
* If you are watching your sodium intake, you can use unsalted butter.
* I used 2% milk and regular cream cheese (not light).

TIPS

* Use a garlic press to mince the garlic for convenience.
* Start cooking the penne first. Make the sauce once the water is boiling and you've added the penne to cook.

Pizza Ravioli

This delightful dish combines cheesy ravioli, marinara sauce, and pizza toppings, baked to perfection for a comforting and flavorful meal.

SERVES: 4 **PREP:** 5 MINUTES **COOK:** 17 MINUTES **TOTAL:** 22 MINUTES

1 pound (500g) fresh ravioli of your choice
5 mild Italian sausages, casings removed
½ cup bacon, uncooked and chopped
1 sweet onion, chopped
1 green bell pepper, chopped
3 cloves garlic, minced
1 jar (about 2 ¾ to 3 cups) marinara sauce
2 teaspoons Italian seasoning
¼ teaspoon black pepper
2 cups mozzarella cheese, shredded

1. Cook the ravioli according to the package directions. Drain and set aside.
2. Add the Italian sausage, bacon, onion, green bell pepper, and garlic to a large skillet over medium heat.
3. Sauté, stirring frequently, for 10 to 12 minutes, or until the sausage and bacon are fully cooked and the vegetables are tender.
4. Stir in the marinara sauce, Italian seasoning, and black pepper. Cook for 4 to 5 minutes, allowing the flavors to meld.
5. Gently stir in the cooked ravioli and shredded mozzarella cheese until well combined and the cheese is melted. Serve hot.

NOTE:

* You can also use frozen ravioli; just follow the package instructions for cooking.
* For a spicier version, substitute mild Italian sausage with hot Italian sausage.
* Use any brand or flavor of pasta sauce you prefer or have on hand.

TIPS

* Ensure your skillet is deep enough to accommodate all the ingredients without spilling.

Cajun Orzo with Sausage

This flavorful and creamy dish combines tender orzo, smoky sausage, and vibrant vegetables with a kick of Cajun seasoning for a comforting and satisfying meal.

SERVES: 4 **PREP:** 10 MINUTES **COOK:** 25 MINUTES **TOTAL:** 35 MINUTES

1 tablespoon extra virgin olive oil
1 ½ cups (12 oz) smoked sausage, sliced
1 yellow onion, chopped
1 red pepper, chopped
1 green pepper, chopped
3 garlic cloves, minced
2 teaspoons Cajun seasoning
½ teaspoon salt
¼ teaspoon black pepper
3 cups chicken broth
1 can (14.5 oz/540 ml) diced tomatoes or stewed tomatoes
2 cups orzo, uncooked
2 cups mozzarella cheese, shredded
½ cup half-and-half cream

1. Heat the extra virgin olive oil in a large, deep skillet over medium heat. Add the sliced sausage, chopped onion, red pepper, green pepper, and minced garlic. Cook for 8 to 10 minutes, stirring occasionally, until the vegetables are softened.
2. Stir in the Cajun seasoning, salt, and black pepper.
3. Add the chicken broth, tomatoes (with their juices), and orzo. Bring to a boil over high heat, then reduce the heat to medium-low and simmer for 10 to 12 minutes, or until the orzo is cooked and has absorbed most of the liquid.
4. Stir in the shredded mozzarella cheese and half-and-half cream. Cook for 1 to 2 minutes or until the cheese is melted and the mixture is creamy. Serve hot.

NOTES

* I used a can of garlic and olive oil petite cut stewed tomatoes. You can also use diced tomatoes or regular stewed tomatoes.

TIPS

* Use a deep skillet to ensure enough room for all the ingredients.
* Add a pinch of cayenne pepper or a splash of hot sauce for an extra kick.

Goulash

Ground beef, macaroni, and rich tomato sauce come together, topped with melted cheddar cheese for a comforting and hearty meal.

SERVES: 6	**PREP:** 10 MINUTES	**COOK:** 35 MINUTES	**TOTAL:** 45 MINUTES

2 pounds lean ground beef
3 cloves garlic, minced
3 tablespoons Worcestershire sauce
1 (28 oz) can diced tomatoes
2 cups tomato sauce
2 cups beef broth
2 cups macaroni, uncooked
1 tablespoon Italian seasoning
3 bay leaves
1 teaspoon paprika
1 teaspoon seasoned salt
¼ teaspoon black pepper
2 cups cheddar cheese, shredded

1. Add the garlic and ground beef to a Dutch oven over medium heat. Stir to break up the beef. Cook for 5 minutes, then add the Worcestershire sauce. Continue to stir frequently for another 5 minutes or until the beef is browned.
2. Add the diced tomatoes, tomato sauce, beef broth, uncooked macaroni, Italian seasoning, bay leaves, paprika, seasoned salt, and black pepper. Stir to combine.
3. Bring the mixture to a boil over high heat. Once boiling, reduce the heat to medium and cook for 20 minutes, stirring often to prevent the macaroni from sticking to the bottom of the pot.
4. Remove the bay leaves carefully using tongs or a spoon. Stir in the shredded cheddar cheese until melted and well combined. Serve hot.

NOTE:

* Remove the bay leaves carefully, as they will be hot.
* You can use regular table salt if you don't have seasoned salt.
* Old cheddar cheese (sharp cheddar) has more flavor than mild cheddar, but either can be used.

TIPS

* Stir often to prevent the macaroni from sticking to the bottom of the Dutch oven.
* Before adding the cheese, test the macaroni noodles to ensure they are cooked to your liking.

Lemon Asparagus Chicken Pasta

This zesty and refreshing dish combines tender chicken, crisp asparagus, and linguine in a light lemon and garlic sauce.

SERVES: 4 **PREP:** 10 MINUTES **COOK:** 15 MINUTES **TOTAL:** 25 MINUTES

1 (16 oz/410 g) package linguine, uncooked
¼ cup unsalted butter
3 chicken breasts, chopped into 1-inch cubes
3 cloves garlic, minced
1 cup chicken broth
1 pound asparagus, trimmed
1 tablespoon lemon juice
Zest of 1 lemon
1 tablespoon fresh thyme (or 1 teaspoon dried thyme)
1 tablespoon Dijon mustard
½ teaspoon salt
¼ teaspoon black pepper
¼ cup Parmesan cheese, grated

1. Cook the linguine according to package directions. Drain and set aside.
2. Melt the butter in a large, deep skillet over medium heat. Add the chicken and garlic and cook for 8 to 10 minutes or until the chicken is cooked.
3. Stir in the chicken broth, asparagus, lemon juice, lemon zest, thyme, Dijon mustard, salt, and black pepper. Bring to a boil over high heat. Once boiling, reduce the heat to medium and continue to cook, stirring often, for 10 minutes or until the asparagus is tender.
4. Remove from heat and stir in the cooked linguine and Parmesan cheese. Serve hot.

NOTES

* If you don't have fresh thyme, use 1 teaspoon of dried thyme.
* Spaghetti or fettuccine can be used instead of linguine.

TIPS

* Use a deep skillet to ensure there's enough room for all the ingredients.
* Start cooking the linguine first to ensure everything is ready at the same time.

Sesame Garlic Ramen Noodles

This dish combines tender ramen noodles with a savory sesame garlic sauce, ginger, and green onions for a quick and flavorful bite.

SERVES: 4 **PREP:** 5 MINUTES **COOK:** 5 MINUTES **TOTAL:** 10 MINUTES

4 (3 oz/85 g) packages of ramen noodles
2 tablespoons toasted sesame oil
4 garlic cloves, minced
1 teaspoon minced ginger
3 green onions, sliced
¼ cup soy sauce
1 teaspoon light brown sugar
Sesame seeds, for garnish, optional

1. Cook the ramen noodles according to package directions, omitting the seasoning packets. Drain and set aside.
2. Heat the toasted sesame oil in a large, deep skillet over medium heat. Add the minced garlic, ginger, and sliced green onions. Sauté for 2 minutes, stirring frequently.
3. In a small bowl, whisk together the soy sauce and light brown sugar. Pour the mixture into the skillet and stir to combine.
4. Add the cooked ramen noodles to the skillet and toss to coat evenly with the sauce. If desired, garnish with sesame seeds and more sliced green onions. Serve hot.

NOTE:

* Do not use the seasoning packets that come with the ramen noodles; you only need the noodles.
* Use minced ginger, not powdered ginger spice. You can buy minced ginger in the produce section or mince fresh ginger yourself.
* If you are concerned about sodium intake, use reduced-sodium soy sauce.

TIPS

* Use a garlic press to mince the garlic quickly and efficiently.
* Use a deep skillet to ensure there's enough room for all the ingredients to mix well.

Chicken

Chicken is such a versatile ingredient, and this chapter is packed with recipes that show just how creative and delicious it can be. Whether you're in the mood for something creamy, tangy, or a little bit indulgent, you'll find a new favorite here.

Start with the **Creamy Pesto Chicken** *(88)* for a dish that's rich, flavorful, and incredibly satisfying. If you're looking for something quick and easy, the **Chicken Caesar Sandwiches** *(91)* are perfect for a tasty dinner that's ready in a flash.

For those nights when you want something comforting yet fresh, the **Tomato Basil Chicken** *(92)* is a lovely, simple option that brings together classic flavors. And if you're feeling adventurous, the **Pizza Stuffed Chicken Breasts** *(94)* are a fun twist on two favorites, combining all the best parts of pizza and chicken into one delicious meal.

The **Baked Honey Mustard Chicken** *(99)* offers a sweet and tangy option that's always a crowd-pleaser, while the **Thai Chicken Noodle Salad** *(100)* brings a burst of vibrant flavors and textures for a light, refreshing dinner.

If you're craving something quick and flavorful, the **Chicken Ramen Stir Fry** *(103)* is an easy, delicious choice that's perfect for busy weeknights. For another pesto-inspired dish, the **Pesto Stuffed Chicken** *(97)* adds a creamy, cheesy surprise that's sure to delight.

The **Lemon Skillet Chicken with Potatoes** *(104)* is a comforting, all-in-one meal that's as easy as it is satisfying, while the **Chicken Thighs with Rosemary and Garlic** *(107)* offer a classic, aromatic dish that fills your kitchen with wonderful scents. And for a little indulgence, the **Bacon Ranch Chicken** *(108)* combines creamy, smoky, and savory flavors for a dinner that's pure comfort food.

These recipes are all about making the most of chicken, turning it into something special without spending hours in the kitchen.

Creamy Pesto Chicken

This dish features tender chicken breasts in creamy pesto sauce, topped with juicy grape tomatoes and Parmesan cheese for an addicting and flavorful bite.

SERVES: 4 **PREP:** 5 MINUTES **COOK:** 43 MINUTES **TOTAL:** 48 MINUTES

¼ cup extra virgin olive oil, divided
4 boneless, skinless chicken breasts seasoned with salt and black pepper
1 sweet onion, chopped
2 cups grape tomatoes
3 cloves garlic, minced
¼ cup all-purpose flour
1 cup chicken broth
¾ cup pesto
½ teaspoon salt
¼ teaspoon black pepper
1 cup half-and-half cream
½ cup Parmesan cheese, grated

1. Heat 2 tablespoons of extra virgin olive oil in a large skillet over medium heat. Add the seasoned chicken breasts and cook for 6 minutes per side until browned. Remove the chicken breasts and set aside.
2. Add 2 tablespoons of extra virgin olive oil in the same skillet. Add the chopped onion, grape tomatoes, and minced garlic. Cook over medium heat for 6 minutes, stirring often, until the vegetables are softened.
3. Sprinkle the all-purpose flour over the vegetable mixture. Stir continuously for 1 minute to cook the flour.
4. Add the chicken broth, pesto, ½ teaspoon salt, and ¼ teaspoon pepper to the skillet. Mix and cook over medium heat for 5 minutes until the sauce thickens.
5. Stir in the half-and-half and grated Parmesan cheese. Cook for 2 minutes, stirring frequently, until the sauce is creamy and smooth.
6. Return the chicken breasts to the skillet, nestling them into the sauce. Spoon some of the sauce over the chicken. Cook for 12 to 15 minutes, stirring occasionally, until the chicken is cooked and reaches an internal temperature of at least 165°F (74°C). Serve hot.

NOTES

* Use the ½ teaspoon salt and ¼ teaspoon pepper for the sauce. Season the chicken with additional salt and pepper to taste before cooking.
* Cherry tomatoes can be used in place of grape tomatoes.

TIPS

* A meat thermometer ensures the chicken is cooked to the proper temperature. It should be at least 165°F (74°C).
* Serve over pasta, rice, or with crusty bread to soak up the delicious sauce.

Chicken Caesar Sandwiches

Warm, toasty garlic bread holds sliced chicken, romaine lettuce, and Caesar dressing for a quick and flavorful sandwich.

SERVES: 2 **PREP:** 2 MINUTES **COOK:** 6 MINUTES **TOTAL:** 8 MINUTES

1 garlic bread loaf, thawed and ready to be baked (baguette style recommended)
2 cooked chicken breasts, sliced
4 cups romaine lettuce, chopped
2 tablespoons Parmesan cheese, grated
2-4 tablespoons Caesar dressing (adjust to taste)

Optional toppings
Cooked crumbled bacon
Marinated sundried tomatoes

1. Preheat the oven to 425°F (220°C).
2. Bake the garlic bread according to the package directions, typically 6-8 minutes. Let it cool slightly before assembling the sandwiches.
3. While the garlic bread is baking, toss the chopped romaine lettuce, Parmesan cheese, and Caesar dressing in a large bowl. If using bacon bits, add them at this step.
4. Once the garlic bread is cool enough to handle, slice it open lengthwise. Layer the bottom half with half the lettuce mixture, followed by sliced chicken and optional toppings like extra bacon or sundried tomatoes. Top with the remaining lettuce mixture.
5. Slice the sandwich in half and serve immediately.

NOTE:

* The garlic bread used in this recipe was baguette-style, baked at 425°F for 6-8 minutes. Adjust the cooking time based on your garlic bread.
* If using a larger garlic bread loaf, this recipe can easily serve 4 people.
* Adjust the amount of Caesar dressing based on your preference. A vinaigrette-style dressing may require less to coat the lettuce evenly.
* You can substitute the chicken with steak if desired for a different flavor.

TIPS

* Ensure the garlic bread is slightly cooled before adding the lettuce mix to prevent the lettuce from wilting.
* Use freshly grated Parmesan cheese for the best flavor

Tomato Basil Chicken

This delicious dish features tender chicken breasts simmered in a savory tomato basil sauce with garlic and Italian seasoning.

SERVES: 4 **PREP:** 10 MINUTES **COOK:** 30 MINUTES **TOTAL:** 40 MINUTES

4 boneless, skinless chicken breasts
¼ cup extra virgin olive oil, divided
2 cups grape tomatoes
4 cloves garlic, minced
1 teaspoon Italian seasoning
⅔ cup chicken broth
½ cup fresh basil, chopped
2 tablespoons red wine vinegar
1 tablespoon tomato paste
½ teaspoon granulated sugar
½ teaspoon salt, plus extra for seasoning the chicken breasts
¼ teaspoon black pepper, plus extra for seasoning the chicken breasts

1. Season the chicken breasts on both sides with salt and pepper.
2. Heat 2 tablespoons of extra virgin olive oil in a large skillet over medium heat. Add the chicken breasts and cook for 6 minutes per side or until golden brown. Remove the chicken from the skillet and place on a plate. Cover with aluminum foil to keep warm.
3. Add 2 tablespoons of extra virgin olive oil in the same skillet. Add the grape tomatoes, garlic, and Italian seasoning. Cook for 2 minutes over medium heat, stirring often.
4. Add the chicken broth, basil, red wine vinegar, tomato paste, granulated sugar, ½ teaspoon salt, and ¼ teaspoon pepper to the skillet. Stir to combine and simmer over medium heat for 3 minutes, stirring often.
5. Return the chicken breasts to the skillet and spoon the sauce over them. Continue to cook over medium heat for 10 minutes or until the chicken reaches an internal temperature of 165°F (74°C). Serve hot.

NOTES

* Use the ½ teaspoon salt and ¼ teaspoon pepper for the sauce. Season the chicken with additional salt and pepper to taste before cooking.
* Cherry tomatoes can be used in place of grape tomatoes.

TIPS

* A meat thermometer ensures the chicken is cooked to the proper temperature. It should be at least 165°F (74°C).
* Serve over pasta, rice, or with a side of crusty bread to soak up the delicious sauce.

Pizza Stuffed Chicken Breasts

This dish features tender chicken breasts stuffed with mozzarella, pepperoni, and fresh basil, all baked to perfection with a savory pizza sauce.

SERVES: 4 **PREP:** 10 MINUTES **COOK:** 20 MINUTES **TOTAL:** 30 MINUTES

4 boneless, skinless chicken breasts
1 teaspoon salt
½ teaspoon black pepper
2 teaspoons garlic powder
2 teaspoons Italian seasoning
1 cup sliced mozzarella cheese
1 cup sliced pepperoni
½ cup fresh basil leaves
1 cup pizza sauce
1 green pepper, diced
1 tablespoon avocado oil

1. Preheat your oven to 425°F (220°C). Slice each chicken breast in half lengthwise, creating a "butterfly". Open the chicken breasts on a sheet of parchment paper. Place another sheet of parchment paper over the chicken and use a mallet or a heavy skillet to pound the chicken to an even thickness, about ¼ inch. Set aside.
2. In a small bowl, combine the salt, pepper, garlic powder, and Italian seasoning. Rub the seasoning mixture evenly over both sides of the chicken breasts.
3. On one side of each chicken breast, layer ¼ cup of pizza sauce, ¼ cup of mozzarella, ¼ cup of pepperoni slices, and ¼ of the diced green pepper. Top with a few fresh basil leaves. Fold the other half of the chicken over the fillings and secure it with 4-5 toothpicks to keep the stuffing in place.
4. Heat an ovenproof large skillet over medium heat and add the avocado oil. Sauté the chicken for 3-4 minutes on each side or until golden brown.
5. Transfer the skillet to the preheated oven and bake for 13-15 minutes or until the chicken reaches an internal temperature of 165°F (74°C).
6. Remove the toothpicks before serving. If desired, top the chicken with extra pizza sauce and cheese.

NOTES

* Be careful not to overstuff the chicken, as it may cause the filling to spill out during cooking. If using smaller chicken breasts, you may need to use less ingredients.
* Top the chicken with extra pizza sauce and cheese before serving to enhance the pizza flavor.
* Serve with pasta, salad, rice, or roasted vegetables.

TIPS

* Use an ovenproof skillet to sear the chicken, making transferring directly into the oven easier.
* Ensure the chicken is evenly pounded to cook uniformly and prevent drying out.

Pesto Stuffed Chicken Breasts

Juicy chicken breasts are stuffed with fresh pesto and melted mozzarella, then baked to perfection and finished with a basil garnish.

SERVES: 4 **PREP:** 5 MINUTE **COOK:** 25 MINUTES **TOTAL:** 30 MINUTES

1 tablespoon avocado oil
4 boneless, skinless chicken breasts
1 teaspoon salt
½ teaspoon black pepper
1 ½ cups pesto (store-bought or home-made)
1 cup fresh mozzarella cheese, sliced
½ cup fresh basil leaves

1. Preheat your oven to 425°F (220°C). Butterfly the chicken breasts by slicing them in half lengthwise, being careful not to cut all the way through.
2. Place the chicken breasts between two large pieces of parchment paper and pound them with a mallet or a heavy skillet until they are an even thickness, approximately ¼ inch thick. Season both sides of the chicken with salt and pepper.
3. Spoon ¼ cup of pesto onto one side of each chicken breast.
4. Top with ¼ cup of sliced mozzarella cheese (add more if you prefer it extra cheesy).
5. Fold the other half of the chicken breast over the filling and secure with toothpicks. Repeat for all chicken breasts.
6. Heat an oven-proof skillet (such as cast iron) over medium heat and add the avocado oil.
7. Sauté the stuffed chicken breasts for 3-4 minutes on each side or until golden brown.
8. Spread the remaining pesto over the tops of the seared chicken breasts and transfer the skillet to the preheated oven and bake for 15 minutes, or until the chicken's internal temperature reaches 165°F (74°C).
9. Remove the toothpicks before serving. Top each chicken breast with fresh basil leaves for garnish.

NOTES

* If you prefer more sauce, feel free to add extra pesto. The size of the chicken breasts will determind how much you add.
* If the toothpicks make searing difficult, trim them to fit the skillet better.
* To ensure even cooking, make sure the chicken breasts are pounded to a uniform thickness.
* Use a meat thermometer to accurately check the internal temperature of the chicken, ensuring it's cooked through.

Baked Honey Mustard Chicken

Chicken breasts baked in a sweet and tangy honey mustard sauce, with hints of rosemary and paprika, making for a tender main dish packed with flavor.

SERVES: 4 **PREP:** 5 MINUTES **COOK:** 40 MINUTES **TOTAL:** 45 MINUTES

4 boneless, skinless chicken breasts
¼ cup honey
2 tablespoons yellow mustard
2 tablespoons wholegrain mustard
1 tablespoon extra virgin olive oil
1 tablespoon fresh rosemary, chopped (or 1 teaspoon dried rosemary)
1 teaspoon paprika
1 teaspoon lemon juice
½ teaspoon salt, plus extra for seasoning chicken
¼ teaspoon pepper, plus extra for seasoning chicken

1. Preheat the oven to 375°F (190°C). Grease a 9x13-inch casserole dish with cooking spray.
2. Season the chicken breasts with salt and pepper. Place them in the casserole dish.
3. In a small mixing bowl, whisk together the honey, yellow mustard, wholegrain mustard, extra virgin olive oil, fresh rosemary, paprika, lemon juice, ½ teaspoon salt, and ¼ teaspoon pepper.
4. Pour the honey mustard mixture over the chicken breasts, ensuring they are well coated. Cover the casserole dish with aluminum foil.
5. Bake in the preheated oven for 20 minutes. Remove the foil, flip the chicken over, and spoon the sauce from the casserole dish over the chicken. Continue baking, uncovered, for 15 to 20 minutes or until the chicken reaches an internal temperature of 165°F (74°C). Serve hot.

NOTE:

* Use the ½ teaspoon salt and ¼ teaspoon pepper in the sauce. Season the chicken with additional salt and pepper to taste.

TIPS

* A meat thermometer ensures the chicken is cooked to the proper temperature. It should be at least 165°F (74°C).
* Serve with roasted vegetables or a side salad for a complete meal.

Thai Chicken Noodle Salad

Chicken, fresh veggies, and ramen noodles come together with a zesty Thai-inspired dressing for a flavorful dish that's great warm or cold.

SERVES: 6 **PREP:** 30 MINUTES **COOK:** 45 MINUTES **TOTAL:** 75 MINUTES

For the Chicken Marinade:

1 pound boneless, skinless chicken breasts

¼ cup soy sauce

1 tablespoon toasted toasted sesame oil

1 tablespoon rice vinegar

1 teaspoon garlic powder

1 teaspoon ginger powder

Thai Noodle Salad Dressing:

¼ cup rice wine vinegar

¼ cup soy sauce

3 tablespoons brown sugar

2 tablespoons toasted toasted sesame oil

1 tablespoon chili garlic sauce (Sambal Oelek)

2 cloves garlic, minced

2 teaspoons fresh ginger, minced

For the Salad:

4 brown rice ramen noodle cakes (or regular ramen noodles)

1 red bell pepper, sliced into strips

1 yellow bell pepper, sliced into strips

1 cup baby spinach

¼ cup raw cashews

¼ cup green onions or cilantro

For the Chicken:

1. In a large bowl, combine the marinade ingredients: soy sauce, toasted sesame oil, rice vinegar, garlic powder, and ginger powder. Add the chicken breasts and toss to coat. Let the chicken marinate for at least 30 minutes, preferably longer (overnight is best for maximum flavor).
2. Preheat the oven to 375°F (190°C). Place the marinated chicken on a baking sheet or in a casserole dish and bake for 40-45 minutes or until the internal temperature reaches 165°F (74°C). Let the chicken rest for 5 minutes, then slice.

For the Salad:

3. Cook the ramen noodles according to the package instructions. Drain and set aside.
4. While the noodles cook, combine the dressing ingredients: rice wine vinegar, soy sauce, brown sugar, toasted sesame oil, chili garlic sauce, minced garlic, and fresh ginger in a large skillet over medium heat. Whisk until the brown sugar is dissolved and the mixture comes to a gentle simmer. Remove from heat and let it cool for a few minutes.
5. In a large serving bowl, combine the cooked noodles, sliced bell peppers, baby spinach, cashews, and sliced chicken. Pour the dressing over the salad and toss to coat evenly.
6. Garnish the salad with chopped green onions or cilantro. Serve warm or cold, depending on your preference.

NOTES

* If you prefer a milder salad, reduce the chili garlic sauce to 2 teaspoons.
* When served warm, the salad has a spicier flavor; the heat diminishes when served cold.

TIPS

* For the best flavor, marinate the chicken overnight.
* Allow the dressing to cool slightly before tossing it with the salad to prevent wilting the spinach too much.

Chicken Ramen Stir Fry

Savory sesame-ginger sauce coats tender chicken, fresh vegetables, and ramen noodles in this quick and easy dinner.

SERVES: 4 **PREP:** 10 MINUTES **COOK:** 25 MINUTES **TOTAL:** 35 MINUTES

3 (3 oz/85 g) packages of ramen noodles
1 tablespoon vegetable oil
2 boneless, skinless chicken breasts, chopped into ½-inch pieces
1 tablespoon toasted sesame oil
1 head of broccoli, cut into florets
1 sweet onion, chopped
1 red pepper, chopped
2 cups sliced cremini mushrooms
3 cloves garlic, minced
1 teaspoon minced ginger
1 (14 to 16 oz) package coleslaw mix, *just the vegetables*
¼ cup soy sauce
2 tablespoons hoisin sauce
1 tablespoon cornstarch
1 tablespoon honey
1 tablespoon rice vinegar
3 green onions, sliced

1. Cook the ramen noodles according to package directions. Discard the seasoning packets. Drain and set aside.
2. Heat the vegetable oil in a large skillet over medium heat. Add the chicken and sauté for 8 to 10 minutes, until the chicken is fully cooked. Remove from the skillet and set aside.
3. In the same skillet, add the toasted sesame oil over medium heat. Add the broccoli, onion, red pepper, mushrooms, garlic, and ginger. Cook for 5 minutes, stirring often.
4. Add the coleslaw mix to the skillet and cook for another 5 minutes, stirring frequently.
5. Return the cooked chicken to the skillet and stir to combine.
6. Whisk together the soy sauce, hoisin sauce, cornstarch, honey, rice vinegar, and green onions in a small bowl. Pour the sauce into the skillet and stir to combine. Cook for 2 to 3 minutes, until the sauce thickens.
7. Add the cooked ramen noodles to the skillet and toss to combine with the chicken and vegetables. Serve hot.

NOTE:

* Discard the spice packs that come with the ramen noodles.
* You can use sliced white button mushrooms instead of cremini mushrooms.
* Minced ginger in the produce section can be used, or you can mince fresh ginger yourself.

TIPS

* Use a large skillet or wok to ensure enough room for all the ingredients.

Lemon Skillet Chicken with Potatoes

This delightful dish features tender chicken breasts, crispy potatoes, and baby carrots cooked in a savory lemon garlic sauce.

SERVES: 4 **PREP:** 10 MINUTES **COOK:** 37 MINUTES **TOTAL:** 47 MINUTES

Salt and pepper, to taste, for seasoning the chicken
¼ cup extra virgin olive oil, divided
4 boneless, skinless chicken breasts
½ pound mini red potatoes, chopped into ½-inch chunks
1 cup baby carrots, chopped
3 cloves garlic, minced
1 cup chicken broth
1 lemon, sliced
½ teaspoon lemon pepper (or regular black pepper)
½ teaspoon salt

1. Season the chicken breasts on both sides with salt and pepper.
2. Heat 2 tablespoons of extra virgin olive oil in a large skillet over medium heat. Add the chicken breasts and cook for 6 minutes per side until golden brown. Remove from the pan and set aside.
3. Add the remaining 2 tablespoons of extra virgin olive oil to the skillet. Add the mini potatoes, carrots, and garlic. Cook for 10 minutes, stirring frequently.
4. Add the chicken broth, lemon slices, lemon pepper, and ½ teaspoon salt to the skillet. Stir to combine.
5. Return the chicken breasts to the skillet. You may need to move the potatoes and carrots around to fit the chicken. Spoon the sauce over the chicken. Cook for another 15 minutes, stirring the potatoes and carrots often, or until the chicken and potatoes are fully cooked. Serve hot.

NOTES

* Use the ½ teaspoon salt and ¼ teaspoon pepper in the sauce. Season the chicken with additional salt and pepper as needed.
* Mini Yukon gold potatoes can be used instead of mini red potatoes.

TIPS

* Stir the potatoes and carrots often to avoid sticking to the pan.
* Chop the potatoes into small pieces to ensure they cook thoroughly. We recommend cutting each potato in half and then into four pieces, making eight pieces per potato.

Chicken Thighs with Rosemary & Garlic

Tender chicken thighs simmered in a simple garlic and rosemary sauce come together for a quick meal the whole family will love.

SERVES: 4 **PREP:** 5 MINUTES **COOK:** 32 MINUTES **TOTAL:** 37 MINUTES

2 tablespoons extra virgin olive oil
8 to 9 boneless, skinless chicken thighs seasoned with salt and pepper
¼ cup chopped shallots
3 cloves garlic, minced
1 tablespoon fresh rosemary, chopped
1 cup chicken broth
½ teaspoon salt
¼ teaspoon black pepper

1. Heat the extra virgin olive oil in a large skillet over medium heat. Add the seasoned chicken thighs and cook for 8 minutes per side until browned. Remove the chicken from the pan and set aside.
2. In the same skillet, add the chopped shallots, minced garlic, and chopped rosemary. Cook for 2 to 3 minutes, stirring often, until the shallots are softened and fragrant.
3. Add the chicken broth, ½ teaspoon salt, and ¼ teaspoon black pepper to the skillet. Stir to combine and cook for 1 to 2 minutes until the mixture is heated.
4. Return the chicken thighs to the skillet, covering them with the sauce. Stir the sauce occasionally and cook for 10 minutes until the chicken is cooked and reaches an internal temperature of 165°F (74°C). Serve hot.

NOTE:

* Use the ½ teaspoon salt and ¼ teaspoon pepper in the sauce. Season the chicken with additional salt and pepper as needed.
* After removing the chicken, the pan should still have oil. If not, you can add more olive oil if needed.
* If you can't find shallots, use a diced sweet onion.

TIPS

* A meat thermometer will help determine if the chicken has reached the proper temperature. It should be at least 165°F (74°C).
* Use a garlic press if you have one to mince the garlic quickly and easily.

Bacon Ranch Chicken

Creamy ranch and sour cream sauce, crispy bacon, and melted cheddar cheese take baked chicken breasts up a level.

SERVES: 4 | **PREP:** 5 MINUTES | **COOK:** 30 MINUTES | **TOTAL:** 35 MINUTES

4 boneless, skinless chicken breasts
½ teaspoon salt
¼ teaspoon black pepper
1 cup Ranch dressing
¾ cup sour cream
2 cups cooked chopped bacon
2 cups shredded cheddar cheese

1. Preheat your oven to 400°F (200°C).
2. Season the chicken breasts with salt and black pepper on both sides, then place them in a 9x13 inch casserole dish.
3. In a medium mixing bowl, stir the Ranch dressing and sour cream until well combined. Pour the mixture over the chicken breasts into the casserole dish.
4. Spread the chopped bacon evenly on top of the chicken. Sprinkle the shredded cheddar cheese over the bacon.
5. Bake in the preheated oven for 25 to 30 minutes or until the chicken reaches an internal temperature of 165°F (74°C). Serve hot.

NOTES

* You can cook the bacon beforehand or use pre-cooked bacon crumbles to save time.
* Serve with rice to soak up the extra sauce.

TIPS

* A meat thermometer will help you determine if the chicken has reached the proper temperature and is ready to eat. It should be at least 165°F (74°C).

Pork

If you're looking to add some variety to your weeknight meals, pork is a fantastic choice—it's versatile, flavorful, and perfect for those busy days when you need dinner on the table fast. This chapter is filled with recipes that highlight the deliciousness of pork, from juicy chops to tender roasts.

Start with the **Ranch Pork Chops and Veggies** *(113)* for a one-pan wonder that's as easy as it is satisfying. If you love the sweet and tangy combo, the **Honey Mustard Pork Chops** *(114)* are sure to be a hit, offering a quick and tasty option that's packed with flavor.

For something a bit more aromatic, the **Garlic Rosemary Pork Chops** *(117)* bring together the earthy flavors of fresh herbs and garlic in a dish that feels both comforting and elegant. And if you're in the mood for something rich and creamy, the **Pork Chops with Mushroom Cream Sauce** *(118)* is a must-try—it's indulgent without being complicated.

The **Pork and Potato Supper** *(121)* is a hearty, all-in-one meal that's perfect for those nights when you want something filling and fuss-free. If you're after a touch of elegance, the **Pork Medallions in Mustard Sauce** *(123)* offers a tender, flavorful dish that feels special but comes together quickly.

Finally, the **Roast Pork with Sweet Potatoes** *(124)* combines tender pork with the natural sweetness of roasted sweet potatoes, making it a perfect comfort meal for any night of the week.

These recipes are all about making pork the star of your dinner table with minimal effort and maximum flavor. So grab your favorite cuts of pork, and let's create some delicious, no-fuss dinners!

Ranch Pork Chops & Veggies

This simple dish features tender pork chops baked alongside seasoned potatoes, green beans, and sweet onions for an easy famliy meal with little clean up.

SERVES: 4 **PREP:** 15 MINUTES **COOK:** 30 MINUTES **TOTAL:** 45 MINUTES

1 ½ pounds mini red potatoes, chopped into ½-inch chunks
2 cups green beans, trimmed
1 sweet onion, sliced
½ cup extra virgin olive oil
2 tablespoons ranch seasoning mix (1 packet)
2 tablespoons lemon juice
3 cloves garlic, minced
½ teaspoon salt
¼ teaspoon black pepper
4 boneless pork chops

1. Preheat the oven to 400°F (200°C). Line a large baking sheet with parchment paper and spray with cooking spray.
2. In a large bowl, toss together the potatoes, green beans, and onion.
3. Whisk together the olive oil, ranch seasoning mix, lemon juice, garlic, salt, and black pepper in a small mixing bowl—reserve 2 tablespoons of the mixture. Pour the remaining mixture over the vegetables and toss to coat.
4. Brush the reserved mixture on both sides of the pork chops.
5. Spread the vegetables and pork chops on the prepared baking sheet in a single layer.
6. Bake for 25 to 30 minutes, or until the pork chops reach an internal temperature of at least 145°F (63°C) and the potatoes are tender.

NOTE:

* We used pork loin center chops in a butterfly cut, but any boneless pork chop will work.
* You can substitute other varieties of mini potatoes for the mini red potatoes.

TIPS

* Chop the potatoes into small, even chunks to ensure they bake completely.
* Use a large baking sheet to fit all the ingredients without overcrowding.

Honey Mustard Pork Chops

Pork chops baked in a savory honey mustard sauce with a hint of paprika and garlic make for a delicous main that's a hit.

SERVES: 4 **PREP:** 5 MINUTES **COOK:** 26 MINUTES **TOTAL:** 31 MINUTES

2 tablespoons extra virgin olive oil
4 boneless pork chops seasoned with salt and pepper
⅓ cup honey
2 tablespoons Dijon mustard
2 tablespoons wholegrain mustard
1 teaspoon paprika
1 teaspoon garlic powder
½ teaspoon salt
¼ teaspoon black pepper

1. Preheat the oven to 350°F (175°C).
2. Heat the extra virgin olive oil in a large skillet over medium heat. Sear the pork chops for 3 minutes on each side until browned. Transfer the pork chops to a 9x13 inch casserole dish.
3. In a small bowl, stir together the honey, Dijon mustard, wholegrain mustard, paprika, garlic powder, ½ teaspoon salt, and ¼ teaspoon black pepper. Pour the mixture over the pork chops in the casserole dish, ensuring they are well coated.
4. Bake in the oven for 20 minutes or until the pork chops' internal temperature reaches 145°F (63°C). Serve hot.

NOTES

* If you are using thicker pork chops, you may need to increase the baking time. A meat thermometer is handy for checking when the pork is cooked correctly.
* We used pork loin center-cut boneless chops, but any boneless pork chop will work.

Garlic Rosemary Pork Chops

This delicious dish features juicy pork chops seasoned with garlic and fresh rosemary, perfectly seared and baked to perfection.

SERVES: 4 **PREP:** 5 MINUTES **COOK:** 16 MINUTES **TOTAL:** 21 MINUTES

¼ cup + 2 tablespoons extra virgin olive oil, divided
4 bone-in pork chops
3 cloves garlic, minced
1 tablespoon fresh rosemary, chopped
½ teaspoon salt
¼ teaspoon black pepper

1. Preheat the oven to 375°F (190°C).
2. Heat 2 tablespoons of extra virgin olive oil in a large oven-proof skillet over medium heat. Sear the pork chops for 3 minutes per side until they are browned.
3. Whisk together ¼ cup extra virgin olive oil, minced garlic, chopped rosemary, salt, and black pepper in a small mixing bowl. Spoon this mixture over the seared pork chops.
4. Transfer the skillet to the preheated oven. Bake for 10 minutes or until the pork chops are fully cooked and reach an internal temperature of 145°F (63°C). Serve hot.

NOTE:

* If you use thicker pork chops, you may need to increase the baking time.
* We used bone-in pork loin center chops, but any boneless or bone-in pork chop will work.

TIPS

* Use a meat thermometer to check for doneness. The internal temperature should be 145°F (63°C).
* Use a garlic press to mince the garlic quickly and easily.

Pork Chops with Mushroom Cream Sauce

Pork chops smothered in a rich mushroom cream sauce with hints of garlic and thyme create a delicious and comforting dish.

SERVES: 4 **PREP:** 10 MINUTES **COOK:** 30 MINUTES **TOTAL:** 40 MINUTES

2 tablespoons extra virgin olive oil
4 boneless pork chops seasoned with salt and black pepper
¼ cup unsalted butter
1 sweet onion, chopped
1 (8 oz/227 g) package of sliced cremini mushrooms
3 cloves garlic, minced
1 tablespoon fresh thyme (or 1 teaspoon dried thyme)
¼ cup all-purpose flour
1 cup chicken broth
1 cup half-and-half cream
1 tablespoon Dijon mustard
½ tablespoon lemon juice
1 teaspoon salt
¼ teaspoon black pepper

1. Heat the extra virgin olive oil in a large skillet over medium heat. Sear the pork chops for 4 minutes per side until browned. Remove from the skillet and set aside.
2. In the same skillet, melt the butter over medium heat. Add the chopped onion, sliced mushrooms, minced garlic, and thyme. Cook for 5 to 6 minutes, stirring often, until the vegetables are softened.
3. Add the flour to the skillet and stir for 1 minute to cook the flour.
4. Stir in the chicken broth, half-and-half, Dijon mustard, lemon juice, salt, and black pepper. Cook over medium heat, stirring often, for 2 minutes until the sauce thickens.
5. Return the pork chops to the skillet, covering them with the sauce. Cook for an additional 10 minutes, stirring the sauce occasionally, until the pork chops are fully cooked and reach an internal temperature of 145°F (63°C). Serve hot.

NOTES

* If you are using thicker pork chops, you may need to increase the baking time. A meat thermometer is handy for checking when the pork is cooked correctly.
* White mushrooms can be used instead of cremini mushrooms.

TIPS

* Serve over rice to soak up the delicious sauce.

Pork and Potato Supper

This hearty meal features a juicy pork loin roast surrounded by tender potatoes, mushrooms, and onions, all roasted to perfection.

SERVES: 4 | **PREP:** 10 MINUTES | **COOK:** 60 MINUTES | **TOTAL:** 70 MINUTES

½ cup + 2 tablespoons extra virgin olive oil, divided
1 pork loin roast (about 3 pound)
2 tablespoons lemon juice
1 tablespoon fresh thyme (or 1 teaspoon dried thyme)
3 cloves garlic, minced
½ teaspoon salt
¼ teaspoon black pepper
1 sweet onion, sliced
1 (8 oz/227 g) package sliced white mushrooms
1 ½ pound mini red potatoes, chopped into quarters

1. Preheat the oven to 350°F (175°C).
2. In a small bowl, whisk together ½ cup extra virgin olive oil, lemon juice, fresh thyme, minced garlic, salt, and black pepper. Spread 2 tablespoons of the mixture all over the pork loin.
3. Heat 2 tablespoons of extra virgin olive oil in a large skillet over medium heat. Sear the pork loin for 4 minutes per side until browned. Transfer the pork loin to a large-rimmed baking sheet.
4. In a large bowl, toss together the sliced onion, mushrooms, and quartered potatoes. Add the remaining marinade mixture to the bowl and toss to combine. Spread the vegetables around the pork loin on the baking sheet.
5. Bake in the preheated oven for 50 minutes or until the pork reaches an internal temperature of at least 145°F (63°C) and the potatoes are tender.
6. Remove from the oven and let the pork rest for 5 to 10 minutes before slicing. Serve hot.

NOTE:

* If you use thicker pork chops, you may need to increase the baking time. A meat thermometer is handy to ensure the pork is cooked correctly.

TIPS

* Use a garlic press to mince the garlic quickly and easily.

Pork Medallions in Mustard Sauce

Pork medallions in a creamy mustard sauce with mushrooms and shallots create a rich and savory dish.

SERVES: 4 **PREP:** 10 MINUTES **COOK:** 30 MINUTES **TOTAL:** 40 MINUTES

¼ cup extra virgin olive oil, divided
1 pork tenderloin, cut into 8 to 12 ½-inch slices
1 (8 oz/227 g) package white button mushrooms, sliced
¼ cup shallots, chopped
3 cloves garlic, minced
1 tablespoon fresh thyme (or 1 teaspoon dried thyme)
1 cup chicken broth
½ cup heavy cream
2 tablespoons wholegrain mustard
2 tablespoons Dijon mustard
1 ½ tablespoons cornstarch
½ teaspoon salt
¼ teaspoon black pepper

1. Heat 2 tablespoons of extra virgin olive oil in a large skillet over medium heat. Sear the pork medallions for 4 minutes per side until browned. Remove from the skillet and set aside.
2. Add 2 tablespoons of extra virgin olive oil to the same skillet. Add the sliced mushrooms, chopped shallots, minced garlic, and thyme. Cook, stirring often, for 3 to 5 minutes until the vegetables are softened.
3. Stir in the chicken broth, heavy cream, wholegrain mustard, Dijon mustard, cornstarch, salt, and black pepper. Cook for 5 minutes, stirring frequently, until the sauce thickens.
4. Return the pork medallions to the skillet, spooning the sauce over them. Cook for an additional 7 to 10 minutes, frequently spooning the sauce over the pork, until the medallions reach an internal temperature of 145°F (63°C). Serve hot.

NOTE:

* If the pork medallions are thicker, you may need to increase the cooking time. A meat thermometer is helpful to ensure the pork is cooked correctly.

TIPS

* Serve over rice to soak up the delicious sauce.

Roast Pork with Sweet Potatoes

This delicious meal features a juicy pork tenderloin and roasted sweet potatoes glazed with a savory maple mustard sauce.

SERVES: 4 **PREP:** 20 MINUTES **COOK:** 45 MINUTES **TOTAL:** 65 MINUTES

4 tablespoons extra virgin olive oil, divided
1 pork tenderloin (1 to 2 pounds)
2 sweet potatoes, peeled and chopped into ½ inch cubes
1 red onion, sliced
¼ cup maple syrup
1 tablespoon Dijon mustard
1 teaspoon garlic powder
1 teaspoon salt
½ teaspoon cinnamon
½ teaspoon chili powder
¼ teaspoon black pepper

1. Preheat the oven to 400°F (200°C).
2. Heat 2 tablespoons of extra virgin olive oil in a large skillet over medium heat. Sear the pork tenderloin for 4 minutes per side until browned. Remove from heat and set aside.
3. In a large bowl, toss the sweet potatoes and red onion together.
4. In a small bowl, whisk together the maple syrup, 2 tablespoons extra virgin olive oil, Dijon mustard, garlic powder, salt, cinnamon, chili powder, and black pepper. Spread 2 tablespoons of the mixture on the pork tenderloin. Pour the remaining mixture over the sweet potatoes and onion, tossing to coat evenly.
5. Spread the coated vegetables on a large-rimmed baking sheet. Bake for 15 minutes.
6. Remove the baking sheet from the oven and move the vegetables to make room for the pork tenderloin in the middle. Return to the oven and bake for 20 minutes or until the pork reaches an internal temperature of 145°F (63°C).
7. Slice the pork tenderloin and serve hot with the roasted sweet potatoes and onion.

NOTES

* You may need to increase the cooking time if you have a larger pork tenderloin. A meat thermometer is helpful to ensure the pork is cooked correctly.

TIPS

* Make sure to chop the sweet potatoes into ½ inch cubes to ensure they cook thoroughly.

Casseroles

When it comes to comfort food, casseroles are hard to beat. They're the kind of dishes that warm your soul, fill your kitchen with delicious aromas, and make dinnertime easy and enjoyable, especially on those busy days. This chapter is all about hearty, satisfying meals that you can throw together with minimal fuss and maximum flavor.

Start with the **Chicken Pot Pie Casserole** *(129)* for a cozy, all-in-one dish that's like a warm hug in every bite. If you're craving something with a little kick, the **Baked Chili Mac and Cheese** *(130)* combines the best of both worlds—rich, cheesy goodness with the comforting flavors of chili.

For a twist on a classic, the **Mexican Chicken Spaghetti Casserole** *(133)* brings together zesty flavors in a dish that's as fun as it is delicious. And if you're a fan of traditional comfort food, the **Baked Macaroni and Cheese** *(134)* is sure to hit the spot with its creamy, cheesy layers.

The **Gnocchi and Sausage Casserole** *(137)* is a satisfying, flavorful option that's perfect for when you want something a little different but still comforting. If you're in the mood for something with a bit of a crunch, the **Chicken Tortilla Casserole** *(138)* offers a delightful combination of textures and tastes.

For a classic, the **Tuna Noodle Casserole** *(141)* brings back all the nostalgic flavors you love, making it a great choice for a family dinner. The **Pepperoni Pizza Gnocchi Bake** *(142)* is a fun, kid-friendly option that combines the best parts of pizza and pasta into one delicious dish.

And finally, the **Chicken Bacon Ranch Bubble-Up Bake** *(145)* is the ultimate comfort food, combining creamy ranch flavors with crispy bacon and tender chicken in a dish that's sure to be a hit with everyone at the table.

These casserole recipes are all about making dinnertime easy, comforting, and delicious. So grab your favorite casserole dish, and dive into some seriously satisfying meals!

Chicken Pot Pie Casserole

This comfort food in a casserole combines tender chicken, mixed vegetables, and a creamy sauce, all topped with a golden crescent roll crust.

SERVES: 4 **PREP:** 10 MINUTES **COOK:** 40 MINUTES **TOTAL:** 50 MINUTES

2 tablespoons unsalted butter
1 sweet onion, chopped
3 celery ribs, chopped
4 cups cooked chicken, chopped into small cubes (approximately 4 chicken breasts)
3 cups frozen mixed vegetables
2 (10.5 oz/284 ml) cans cream of chicken soup
1 teaspoon garlic powder
½ teaspoon dried thyme (or 1 tablespoon fresh thyme)
½ teaspoon salt
¼ teaspoon black pepper
1 (8 oz/235 g) can crescent roll dough (I used Pillsbury)

1. Preheat the oven to 350°F (175°C). Grease a 9x13-inch casserole dish with cooking spray.
2. Melt the butter in a large skillet over medium heat. Add the chopped onion and celery, and cook for 6 to 8 minutes, until the vegetables are softened. Remove from heat.
3. Mix the cooked chicken, sautéed onions and celery, frozen mixed vegetables, cream of chicken soup, garlic powder, thyme, salt, and black pepper in a large bowl.
4. Spread the mixture evenly in the prepared casserole dish. Layer the crescent roll dough on top of the chicken mixture.
5. Bake in the oven for 30 minutes or until the top is golden brown. Serve hot.

NOTE:

* Salted butter can be used instead of unsalted butter, but you may want to reduce the salt in the recipe to ¼ teaspoon.
* The frozen mixed vegetables do not need to be thawed before using.
* Do not add water to the soup; use it straight from the can.

TIPS

* Use leftover chicken or a cooked rotisserie chicken from the grocery store to save time.

Baked Chili Mac & Cheese

This delicious dish combines creamy mac and cheese with savory chili, all baked to perfection with a crispy breadcrumb topping.

SERVES: 6 | **PREP:** 2 MINUTES | **COOK:** 30 MINUTES | **TOTAL:** 32 MINUTES

4 cups uncooked macaroni
2 tablespoons salted butter
2 tablespoons all-purpose flour (see notes for gluten-free option)
1 cup milk (I used 2%)
½ cup half-and-half cream
½ cup cream cheese cut into cubes
2 cups cheddar cheese, divided
¾ cup Gruyere cheese, divided (½ cup and ¼ cup)
1 teaspoon garlic powder
½ teaspoon paprika
¼ teaspoon nutmeg
¼ teaspoon ground black pepper
½ to 1 cup pasta water
1 (15 oz) can vegetarian chili (or 1 ½ cups homemade chili)
⅓ to ½ cup breadcrumbs

NOTES

* You can use a 9x13 inch casserole dish or the same oven-proof skillet to make the cheese sauce for baking the chili mac and cheese.

GLUTEN FREE TIPS

* Substitute all-purpose flour with brown rice flour for the roux, gluten-free macaroni and gluten-free breadcrumbs.

* Cook the macaroni for 2-3 minutes less than the package directions for al dente (I used 4 minutes for the Barilla brand).

1. Preheat the oven to 375°F (190°C). Bring a pot of salted water to a boil and cook the macaroni for 1-2 minutes, less than the package instructions for al dente. Reserve 1 cup of pasta water, then drain and rinse the macaroni under cold water to stop cooking.
2. While the macaroni is cooking, melt the butter in a large oven-proof skillet over medium heat.
3. Add the flour and whisk constantly for 1-2 minutes until the mixture has a sandy texture. Gradually whisk in the milk and half-and-half, continuing to whisk until the mixture is smooth and heated through.
4. Reduce the heat to medium-low and add the cream cheese cubes, whisking until melted and the sauce thickens, about 1 minute.
5. Stir 1 cup of cheddar cheese, ½ cup of Gruyere, garlic powder, paprika, nutmeg, and pepper. Whisk until fully combined and bubbly, about 2-3 minutes.
6. Add the cooked macaroni noodles to the skillet, along with ½ cup of the reserved pasta water, and stir to combine. If the mixture is too thick, gradually add more pasta water, a little at a time, until the desired consistency is reached.
7. Spoon the chili over the mac and cheese. Top with the remaining 1 cup of cheddar cheese ¼ cup of Gruyere, and sprinkle with breadcrumbs.
8. Bake for 20-25 minutes until the cheese is bubbly and the breadcrumbs are golden brown. Serve immediately.

Mexican Chicken Spaghetti Casserole

This easy casserole combines tender chicken, spaghetti, and a zesty blend of ROTEL® tomatoes, sour cream, and taco seasoning, all topped with melted cheddar cheese.

SERVES: 6 **PREP:** 10 MINUTES **COOK:** 45 MINUTES **TOTAL:** 55 MINUTES

8 oz spaghetti, uncooked
2 tablespoons extra virgin olive oil
1 sweet onion, chopped
3 cloves garlic, minced
2 cups cooked chicken, cut into small cubes (approximately 2 chicken breasts)
2 (10 oz/284 ml) cans ROTEL® diced tomatoes and green chilies
1 cup sour cream
1 tablespoon taco seasoning
2 cups shredded cheddar cheese

1. Preheat the oven to 350°F (175°C). Grease a 9x13-inch casserole dish and set aside.
2. Cook the spaghetti according to package directions. Drain and set aside.
3. Heat the extra virgin olive oil in a large skillet over medium heat. Add the chopped onion and minced garlic. Cook for 5 to 7 minutes or until the onions are softened.
4. In a large bowl, stir the cooked spaghetti, chicken, sautéed onions and garlic, ROTEL®, sour cream, and taco seasoning. Spread the mixture evenly in the prepared casserole dish.
5. Cover the casserole with aluminum foil. Bake in the preheated oven for 30 minutes.
6. Remove the foil. Top the casserole with shredded cheddar cheese. Return the casserole to the oven, uncovered, and bake for 5 minutes or until the cheese is melted. Serve hot.

NOTE:

* 8 oz of dry spaghetti yields about 2 cups of cooked spaghetti. If measuring dry spaghetti, 8 oz should be about 1 ½ inches in diameter when held in a bundle.
* You can use another brand of diced tomatoes with green chilies if you can't find ROTEL®.

TIPS

* Use leftover chicken or a cooked rotisserie chicken from the grocery store to save time.

Baked Macaroni & Cheese

This comfort food favorite features tender elbow macaroni baked in a rich cheddar cheese sauce, topped with a crispy panko breadcrumb crust.

SERVES: 6 **PREP:** 20 MINUTES **COOK:** 20 MINUTES **TOTAL:** 40 MINUTES

16 oz elbow macaroni, uncooked (about 454 g)
½ cup + 2 tablespoons unsalted butter, divided
⅓ cup all-purpose flour
2 cups milk (I used 2%)
2 cups half-and-half cream
½ teaspoon salt
½ teaspoon mustard powder
¼ teaspoon black pepper
2 cups sharp cheddar cheese, shredded
2 cups panko breadcrumbs

1. Preheat the oven to 350°F (175°C). Grease a 9x13 inch casserole dish and set aside.
2. Cook the elbow macaroni according to package directions until al dente. Drain and set aside.
3. Melt ½ cup (1 stick) of butter in a large saucepan over medium heat. Add the flour and stir constantly for 1 minute to form a roux.
4. Gradually stir in the milk, half-and-half, salt, mustard powder, and black pepper. Turn the heat to high and cook, stirring frequently, until the mixture thickens (about 5 to 8 minutes). Remove from heat.
5. Stir in the shredded cheddar cheese until thoroughly melted and combined.
6. Add the cooked elbow macaroni to the cheese sauce and stir to combine. Spread the mixture evenly in the prepared casserole dish.
7. Melt the remaining 2 tablespoons of butter. Mix the melted butter with the panko breadcrumbs in a medium bowl and stir to coat evenly.
8. Spread the breadcrumb mixture evenly on top of the macaroni. Bake in the oven for 20 minutes or until the breadcrumbs are golden brown. Serve hot.

NOTES

* Use a 16 oz (454 g) package of elbow macaroni.
* I used sharp cheddar (old cheddar) in this recipe for extra flavor.

TIPS

* Cook the macaroni to al dente to ensure it doesn't overcook in the oven.
* To make it gluten free: substitute all-purpose flour with brown rice flour, gluten-free macaroni and gluten-free panko breadcrumbs.

Gnocchi and Sausage Casserole

This hearty casserole features tender gnocchi, savory Italian sausage, and vibrant vegetables, all baked in a rich marinara sauce with a melty mozzarella topping.

SERVES: 6 **PREP:** 5 MINUTES **COOK:** 30 MINUTES **TOTAL:** 35 MINUTES

1 pound hot Italian sausage, casings removed
1 yellow onion, diced
1 green pepper, diced
1 red pepper, diced
2 cups baby spinach
3 cups jarred marinara sauce
½ cup chicken broth
1 kg gnocchi (2 x 500g packages or 2.2 pounds)
1 ½ cups shredded mozzarella cheese
2-3 tablespoons fresh basil, sliced

1. Preheat the oven to 375°F (190°C) and spray a 9x13 inch casserole dish with olive oil spray.
2. In a large skillet over medium heat, cook the hot Italian sausage, breaking it into crumbles, until almost fully cooked, about 3-4 minutes.
3. Add the diced onion and peppers to the skillet. Continue to sauté until the onions are translucent and the peppers are softened about 5-7 minutes. Stir in the baby spinach and cook until wilted.
4. Stir in the marinara sauce, chicken broth, and gnocchi, ensuring everything is well combined.
5. Transfer the mixture to the prepared casserole dish. Sprinkle the shredded mozzarella cheese evenly over the top.
6. Cover the casserole dish with foil and bake for 10 minutes. Remove the foil and bake for 10 minutes or until the cheese is melted and bubbly.
7. Remove from the oven and sprinkle the fresh basil over the top before serving.

NOTE:

* I used gluten-free gnocchi for this recipe, but regular gnocchi will also work.
* If you prefer a milder flavor, you can substitute the hot Italian sausage with mild or sweet Italian sausage.

TIPS

* Make sure to evenly distribute the gnocchi in the casserole dish to ensure even cooking.
* For added flavor, consider topping the casserole with a sprinkle of Parmesan cheese before baking.

Chicken Tortilla Casserole

A flavorful casserole with layers of tender chicken, corn tortillas, and a zesty sauce, all crowned with melted cheddar cheese.

SERVES: 6 **PREP:** 10 MINUTES **COOK:** 55 MINUTES **TOTAL:** 65 MINUTES

1 tablespoon extra virgin olive oil
1 sweet onion, chopped
1 green pepper, chopped
1 (15 oz/540 ml) can black beans, drained and rinsed
1 (10 oz/284 ml) can ROTEL® diced tomatoes and green chilies
1 cup chicken broth
1 teaspoon cumin
1 teaspoon chili powder
1 teaspoon garlic powder
½ teaspoon dried oregano
½ teaspoon salt
8 (6-inch) corn tortillas, divided
5 cups shredded cooked chicken, divided
2 cups shredded cheddar cheese, divided

1. Preheat the oven to 375°F (190°C). Grease a 9x13 inch casserole dish.
2. Heat the olive oil in a large pot over medium heat. Add the chopped onion and green pepper, and cook for 8 to 10 minutes, stirring frequently, until the vegetables are softened.
3. Stir in the black beans, ROTEL®, chicken broth, cumin, chili powder, garlic powder, dried oregano, and salt. Cook over medium heat for 10 minutes, stirring occasionally.
4. Spread a thin layer of the sauce on the bottom of the prepared casserole dish and layer 4 corn tortillas on top.
5. Layer 2 ½ cups of shredded chicken on top of the tortillas.
6. Add half of the remaining sauce on top of the chicken.
7. Layer 1 cup of shredded cheddar cheese on top of the sauce.
8. Add another layer of 4 corn tortillas on top of the cheese.
9. Layer the remaining 2 ½ cups of shredded chicken on the tortillas.
10. Layer the remaining sauce on top of the chicken.
11. Top with the remaining 1 cup of shredded cheddar cheese.
12. Cover with aluminum foil and bake for 30 minutes.
13. Remove the foil and bake for 5 minutes until the cheese is melted and bubbly. Let the casserole sit for 5 minutes before cutting into pieces and serving.

NOTES

* If you can't find ROTEL®, use another brand of diced tomatoes and green chilies; you'll need 1 ¼ cups.
* If you prefer, you can use flour tortillas instead of corn tortillas.
* If you can't find 6-inch tortillas, you can use a different size and adjust the number of tortillas accordingly.

TIPS

* Use leftover chicken or a cooked rotisserie chicken from the grocery store to save time.
* 5 cups of shredded chicken equals about 5 chicken breasts or 3 large chicken breasts.

Tuna Noodle Casserole

This classic casserole combines tender egg noodles, savory tuna, and a creamy sauce, topped with crispy fried onions for a delightful crunch.

SERVES: 4 **PREP:** 10 MINUTES **COOK:** 35 MINUTES **TOTAL:** 45 MINUTES

3 cups egg noodles, uncooked
¼ cup salted butter, divided
1 sweet onion, diced
2 cloves garlic, minced
¼ cup all-purpose flour
2 cups half-and-half cream
1 cup milk
½ teaspoon salt
¼ teaspoon black pepper
½ cup frozen peas
2 (5 oz/170 g) cans tuna, drained

Topping

1 cup crispy fried onions, crushed
1 tablespoon melted salted butter

1. Preheat the oven to 350°F (175°C). Grease a 9x13-inch casserole dish with cooking spray.
2. Cook the egg noodles according to package directions until al dente. Drain and set aside.
3. Heat 1 tablespoon of butter in a skillet over medium heat. Add the onions and garlic and cook for 6 to 8 minutes, until the onions are softened. Remove from heat and set aside.
4. Heat the remaining 3 tablespoons of butter in a large saucepan over medium heat. Add the flour and cook for 1 minute, stirring constantly. Increase the heat to high and whisk in the half-and-half and milk. Whisk continually until the mixture thickens, about 5 minutes. Remove from heat.
5. Add salt, black pepper, cooked egg noodles, frozen peas, tuna, garlic, and onion to the sauce mixture and stir to combine. Spread the mixture evenly in the prepared casserole dish.
6. In a small bowl, stir together the crushed crispy fried onions and melted butter. Spread the topping evenly over the tuna mixture in the casserole dish.
7. Bake in the oven for 20 minutes or until the casserole is hot and bubbly. Serve hot.

NOTE:

* Crispy fried onions are usually found with the croutons in the grocery store and are often used as a salad topper. Use panko breadcrumbs or crushed cornflakes instead if you can't find them.

TIPS

* To crush the crispy fried onions, place them in a zip-top bag and roll over them with a rolling pin to crush.

Pepperoni Pizza Gnocchi Bake

This casserole is a twist on a dinner time favorite. Featuring tender gnocchi, savory sausage, pepperoni, and mushrooms in a rich tomato sauce, all topped with melted mozzarella cheese.

SERVES: 6 **PREP:** 5 MINUTES **COOK:** 35 MINUTES **TOTAL:** 40 MINUTES

2 pounds potato gnocchi, uncooked
4 mild Italian sausages, casings removed
1 (8 oz/227 g) package sliced white button mushrooms
3 garlic cloves, minced
1 (28 oz) can crushed tomatoes
1 cup pepperoni slices, divided
1 teaspoon Italian seasoning
½ teaspoon salt
¼ teaspoon black pepper
2 cups shredded mozzarella cheese

1. Preheat the oven to 375°F (190°C). Spray a 9x13-inch casserole dish with cooking spray.
2. Cook the gnocchi according to the package directions. Drain and set aside.
3. Add the sausage, mushrooms, and garlic to a large skillet. Cook over medium heat, stirring often to break up the sausage, until the sausage is cooked through, about 8 to 10 minutes. Remove from heat.
4. Stir in the cooked gnocchi, crushed tomatoes, ½ cup pepperoni slices, Italian seasoning, salt, and black pepper. Mix well to combine.
5. Spread the mixture into the prepared casserole dish. Top with shredded mozzarella cheese and the remaining ½ cup of pepperoni slices.
6. Cover the casserole dish with aluminum foil and bake for 20 minutes. Remove the foil and bake for 5 minutes or until the cheese is melted and bubbly. Serve hot.

NOTES

* Use hot Italian sausage if you prefer a spicier dish.

TIPS

* Ensure the gnocchi is well-drained before adding it to the mixture to avoid excess moisture in the casserole.

Chicken Bacon Ranch Bubble-Up Bake

This bake combines tender chicken, crispy bacon, and fluffy biscuit pieces, all smothered in creamy ranch dressing and topped with melted cheddar cheese.

SERVES: 4 **PREP:** 10 MINUTES **COOK:** 30 MINUTES **TOTAL:** 40 MINUTES

4 cups cooked chicken, chopped into small cubes
8 slices cooked bacon, chopped
1 ½ cups Ranch dressing
1 can refrigerated biscuits, unbaked, cut into quarters (I used Pillsbury)
2 cups shredded cheddar cheese

1. Preheat the oven to 350°F (175°C). Grease a 9x13-inch casserole dish with cooking spray.
2. In a large bowl, stir together the cooked chicken, chopped bacon, and Ranch dressing. Spread the mixture evenly in the prepared casserole dish.
3. Spread the quartered pieces of refrigerated biscuit dough on top of the chicken mixture.
4. Bake in the preheated oven for 25 minutes.
5. Remove from the oven and sprinkle the shredded cheddar cheese evenly over the top. Return to the oven and bake for 5 minutes or until the cheese is melted and bubbly. Serve hot.

NOTE:

* Any variety of refrigerated biscuits should work fine.

TIPS

* Cook the chicken and bacon ahead of time and store them in the fridge to save on prep time.
* Ensure the biscuit pieces are evenly spread out to ensure even cooking.

A Big Thank You to You & a Gift!

We're so excited that you've chosen The Busy Day Dinners Cookbook to join you on your cooking adventures! It really means a lot to us that you're inviting us into your kitchen.

This isn't just a cookbook; it's a piece of our love for cooking, and knowing it might inspire your meals means the world to us.

To show our appreciation, we're thrilled to give you free access to the Ultimate Dinner Planning Pack! Simply scan the QR code for instructions on how to get your copy or you can visit https://busydaydinners.com/bddgift.

Thank you for your support.
- Randa and Stacie

Acknowledgements

We are deeply grateful to our incredible recipe testers for their invaluable feedback and support throughout the creation of this cookbook.

A heartfelt thank you goes to Lyne Proulx, Louise Edington, Candace Gwinn, Shawna Snider, Tara Noland, Rachel Henry, Mandy Gorr, Eva Filer, Christina Rose, Tammy Bell, Jillian Bimm, Jenn Glover, Christelle Proulx, Carolann Hughes, Karina Roux, and Cyn Gagen.

Your insights and dedication have been instrumental in bringing these recipes to life, making this book a true labor of love. Thank you for being a part of this journey with us.

Index

www.ingramcontent.com/pod-product-compliance
Ingram Content Group UK Ltd.
Pitfield, Milton Keynes, MK11 3LW, UK
UKHW062007290726
14090UKWH00022B/1427